Crime And Criminals

INQUIRY INTO CRUCIAL AMERICAN PROBLEMS

Series Editor · JACK R. FRAENKEL

Crime And Criminals:

What Should We Do About Them?

JACK R. FRAENKEL

Associate Professor of
Interdisciplinary Studies in Education
San Francisco State College

PRENTICE-HALL, INC.   ENGLEWOOD CLIFFS, N.J.

Titles in this series:

CRIME AND CRIMINALS: What Should We Do About Them?
Jack R. Fraenkel

PREJUDICE AND DISCRIMINATION: Can We Eliminate Them?
Fred R. Holmes

THE DRUG SCENE: Help or Hang-up?
Walter L. Way

POVERTY IN AN AFFLUENT SOCIETY: Personal Problem or National Disgrace?
David A. Durfee

COUNTRY, CONSCIENCE, AND CONSCRIPTION: Can They Be Reconciled?
Leo A. Bressler and Marion A. Bressler

VOICES OF DISSENT: Positive Good or Disruptive Evil?
Frank Kane

CITIES IN CRISIS: Decay or Renewal?
Rudie W. Tretten

TEEN-AGERS AND SEX: Revolution or Reaction?
Jack L. Nelson

PROPAGANDA, POLLS, AND PUBLIC OPINION: Are the People Manipulated?
Malcolm G. Mitchell

ALIENATION: Individual or Social Problem?
Ronald V. Urick

EDUCATION AND OPPORTUNITY: For What and For Whom?
Gordon M. Seely

FOREIGN POLICY: Intervention, Involvement, or Isolation?
Alvin Wolf

© Copyright 1970 by Prentice-Hall, Inc.,
Englewood Cliffs, N.J.
All rights reserved. No part
of this book may be
reproduced in any form
or by any means
without permission
in writing from the publisher.

Printed in the United States of America

13-192898-8 paper
13-192906-2 cloth

1 2 3 4 5 6 7 8 9 10

Prentice-Hall International, Inc.,
London
Prentice-Hall of Australia, Pty. Ltd.,
Sydney
Prentice-Hall of Canada, Ltd.,
Toronto
Prentice-Hall of India Private Ltd.,
New Delhi
Prentice-Hall of Japan, Inc.,
Tokyo

PREFACE

The series *INQUIRY INTO CRUCIAL AMERICAN PROB-LEMS* focuses upon a number of important contemporary social and political issues. Each book presents an in-depth study of a particular problem, selected because of its pressing intrusion into the minds and consciences of most Americans today. A major concern has been the desire to make the materials relevant to students. Every title in the series, therefore, has been selected because, in one way or another, it suggests a problem of concern to students today.

A number of divergent viewpoints, from a wide variety of different *kinds* of sources, encourage discussion and reflection and illustrate that the same problem may be viewed from many different vantage points. Of concern throughout is a desire to help students realize that honest men may legitimately differ in their views.

After a short chapter introducing the questions with which the book will deal, Chapter 2 presents a brief historical and contemporary background so that students will have more than just a superficial understanding of the problem under study. In the readings that follow, a conscientious effort has been made to avoid endorsing any one viewpoint as the "right" viewpoint, or to evaluate the arguments of particular individuals. No conclusions are drawn. Instead, a number of questions for discussion and reflection are posed at the end of each reading so that students can come to their own conclusions.

Great care has been taken to insure that the readings included in each book are just that—readable! We have searched particularly for articles that are of high interest, yet from which differing viewpoints may be legitimately inferred. Whenever possible, dialogues involving or descriptions showing actual people responding and reacting to problematic situations are presented. In sum, each book

- presents divergent, conflicting views on the problem under consideration;

- gives as many perspectives and dimensions on the problem as space permits;

- presents articles on a variety of reading levels, in order to appeal to students of many different ability levels;

- presents analytical as well as descriptive statements;

- deals with real people involved in situations of concern to them;

- includes questions which encourage discussion and thought of the various viewpoints expressed;

- includes activities to involve students to consider further the issues embedded in the problem.

CONTENTS

Introduction

Mrs. Robert Foster, a thirty-year-old telephone operator, mother of two children, bends over to look at a flat tire on her car in a Saint Louis parking lot, shortly after leaving work around six o'clock of a December evening. She is struck on the head with a baseball bat; her unconscious body is dragged into a backyard by two boys, one seventeen, one sixteen. They rape her; she dies. . . . Catherine Nellen, age fifteen, gets on a bus in a Milwaukee suburb to go to a Junior Achievement meeting; the only other passenger is a man, who, without warning, seizes her from behind and cuts her throat with a razor, severing the jugular vein; she dies. . . . A woman nurse walks to her car in the Dorchester section of Boston, in midevening, after a church dance; two young men and two girls force her, at gunpoint, to take them in her car; she is found in the morning, many miles away, at the side of the Maine Turnpike, brutally pistol-whipped. . . . An elderly Bronx widow, inserting her key into the door of her fifth-floor apartment, is attacked from behind by a hoodlum, who snatches her bag, then throws her down a flight of stairs. The same woman, after recovering, shops in a supermarket at four o'clock one afternoon. A man grabs for her purse. Determined not to be robbed again, she holds on to it tightly and screams. The thief smashes her in the face with his fist and beats her to the ground, while other shoppers stare. She lets go; the man takes the purse and leaves.*

Crime is riding high, wide, and ugly today in many parts of the United States. Robberies, arson, assault, and homicide all are on the increase. The FBI has stated in its Uniform Crime Reports that the crime

---

* Excerpted from Samuel Grafton, "The Crime That Threatens Every Woman," *McCall's Magazine,* February 1965. Copyright 1965 *McCall's Magazine.* Reprinted by permission McCall Corporation, Inc.

rate is increasing five to six times as fast as our population! In 1964, over 2½ million serious crimes, such as homicide, robbery, aggravated assault, burglary, and auto theft, were reported to police. In 1965, there were more than 5,600 murders, 34,700 aggravated assaults with a gun, and over 68,400 armed robberies.

Although the pattern of any given crime will vary, the chart below indicates one day of robberies in Washington, D.C., in December of 1966. Though this admittedly is extraordinary, it should give you some idea of how many crimes can occur in a single day, as well as indicate how costly crime can be.

ONE DAY OF CRIME *

The pattern of a crime like robbery is, of course, irregular. A rash of robberies at a single time may give people the feeling that they are engulfed by danger and lawlessness. In Washington, D.C., for example, between 8 A.M., Friday, December 9, and 8 A.M., Saturday, December 10, 1966, an extraordinary total of 35 robberies that netted the robbers almost $16,000 was reported to the Metropolitan Police Department.

Friday, December 9:

9:15 A.M.	Strongarm robbery, street, $2.
10:00 A.M.	Armed robbery, liquor store, $1,500.
11:30 A.M.	Pocketbook snatched with force and violence, street, $3.
12:30 P.M.	Holdup with revolver, roofing company, $2,100.
2:40 P.M.	Holdup with gun, shoe store, $139.
3:20 P.M.	Holdup with gun, apartment, $92.
4:55 P.M.	Holdup with gun, bank, $8,716.
6:25 P.M.	Mugging, street, $5.
6:50 P.M.	Holdup with revolver, tourist home, $30.
7:00 P.M.	Strongarm robbery, street, $25.
7:05 P.M.	Holdup with gun, auto in parking lot, $61.
7:10 P.M.	Strongarm robbery, apartment house, $3.
7:15 P.M.	Holdup with revolver (employee shot twice), truck rental company, $200.
7:25 P.M.	Mugging, street, $5.
7:50 P.M.	Holdup with gun, transfer company, $1,400.
8:55 P.M.	Holdup with shotgun, newspaper substation, $100.
10:10 P.M.	Holdup with gun, hotel, $289.50.
10:15 P.M.	Strongarm robbery, street, $120.
10:30 P.M.	Holdup with gun, street, $59.50.
10:53 P.M.	Strongarm robbery, street, $175.
11:05 P.M.	Holdup, tavern, $40.
11:30 P.M.	Strongarm robbery, street, $3.
11:55 P.M.	Strongarm robbery, street, $51.

Saturday, December 10:

12:20 A.M.	Strongarm robbery, street, $19.	
1:10 A.M.	Strongarm robbery, apartment house, $3.	
3:25 A.M.	Strongarm robbery, street, $25.	
3:50 A.M.	Holdup with knife, street, $23.	
3:55 A.M.	Holdup with gun, street, $25.	
4:20 A.M.	Robbery with intent to rape, street, 75 cents.	
4:20 A.M.	Holdup with gun, carryout shop, $80.	
6:25 A.M.	Holdup-rape, street, $20.	
6:25 A.M.	Holdup with gun, tourist home, no amount listed.	
6:45 A.M.	Holdup, street, $5.	
7:30 A.M.	Holdup with knife, cleaners, $300.	
7:40 A.M.	Strongarm robbery, street, $80.	

* The President's Crime Commission.

But this is not all. In the first nine months of 1967, the nation's crime rate increased 16 per cent over the same period in 1966. The highest percentage increase—17 per cent—was in suburban communities. Big cities registered an overall 15 per cent crime rise and rural areas 12 per cent. During the first nine months of 1968, the overall increase was 19 per cent over the same period in 1967.

The situation may be even more alarming than this, however. A nationwide survey by the University of Chicago's Opinion Research Center found that there is *twice* as much crime in the United States as the FBI's periodic reports indicate. Focusing upon the same crimes used by the FBI for its Uniform Crime Reports—homicide, forcible rape, robbery, aggravated assault, burglary, larceny (of more than $50.00), and car theft—the study found the "true" crime rate in the United States to be 2119.6 offenses per 100,000 population! The FBI for the same year (1965) reported a rate of 947.7 per 100,000. In some categories the difference was even greater.

The researchers questioned a nationwide cross-section sample of 10,-000 Americans. The FBI, in contrast, accumulates its data from police reports. The discrepancy seems to indicate that many crimes are not reported to the police. This is borne out by the Crime Commission survey: Only 49 per cent of the offenses recalled by the victims were reported to the police. Here were some of the reasons they offered:

· It wasn't a police matter (34 per cent); that is, the offender was a relative, lover, or friend, and the victim didn't want police intervention.

· The victim feared reprisal (2 per cent).

· The victim didn't know how to enlist police aid (9 per cent).

· The victim didn't like, trust, or believe in the effectiveness of the police (55 per cent).

On the other hand, many people believe that the crime crisis has been exaggerated. Some state that more accurate reporting and better record keeping may account for some of the apparent increase. The last reading in this book expresses this opinion. As you read, you will have the opportunity to weigh these opposing points of view, as well as consider these important questions in depth:

1. What do we mean by crime?
2. Has crime always existed?
3. What causes crime?
4. How should the police deal with crime and criminals?
5. How should society approach the problem of crime?
6. Can crime be eliminated?

These, of course, are only some of the questions which might be asked about the nature of crime. A variety of viewpoints and facts dealing with each topic follows, to provide you with a basis for discussion and for arriving at your own conclusions concerning the problem of crime in American society today.

2

Has Crime Always Existed?

How long has crime been with us? Is it a recent phenomenon or has it always existed? Has the meaning of "crime" changed over time? This chapter presents a brief history of crime which may help you to draw some conclusions about these questions.

Crime in the Past

To early man crime was the violation of taboo. Living in a very small family group, this ultra-individualist fought fiercely to defend his feeding grounds and to protect his mate from being carried off by others. As time passed, however, he, along with other men, began to travel in bands of families (clans or tribes) headed by a leader or patriarch who wielded supreme power and ultimate control over the disposition of the females of the clan. Stirred perhaps by jealousy and perhaps by a longing for power in their own right, other powerful individuals in the clan, often the patriarch's own sons, challenged his power. Attempts to kill the leader were frequent, and many times they succeeded.

In time, this murder of the leader became taboo, or forbidden, and when his days of strength were over, the leader was allowed to abdicate. His personal murder was replaced by the slaying of an animal. The notion of "guilt" developed from this injunction against murdering the leader of the tribe. Fear for their own fate restrained the sons. And a custom was born.

Customs are accepted patterns of behavior that have developed through long usage and uniform practice. Their violation frequently brings considerable social disapproval; consequently, they can be a powerful influence in regulating behavior. For example, in the past certain communities in South America had no law or law courts but instead relied solely on public opinion to regulate behavior. Similarly, crime was such a rare thing among the Iroquois Indians that a penal code was not necessary. Societies like these are strongly controlled by custom.

As time passed, early man found his life governed more and more by custom, taboo, and myth. The authority which the all-powerful leader of the tribe had possessed became transferred to local rulers or to the many gods conceived by men to explain the occurrences in the world which they could not understand. It was an accepted fact that certain things could be done and certain things could not.

Retribution and vengeance for acts committed by one individual against another (such as wife-stealing, cattle theft, or murder) were personal. In many early societies each man was his own policeman and administered his own vengeance. The murder of Og by Thur would lead to Thur's murder by Og's son or friend Tok, and then Tok's murder by one of Thur's relatives, and on and on. In ancient Babylonia if one man broke another man's bones, his own bones were broken. This idea of revenge plays a large part in the Mosaic Code, which demands a "life for life, eye for eye, tooth for tooth, hand for hand, foot for foot. . . ."

The Abyssinians decreed that when a boy fell from a tree upon the neck of his friend and killed him, the dead boy's brother should be sent into the tree to fall upon the culprit's neck. The famous law code of Hammurabi, King of Babylonia from 2123–2081 B.C., decreed that if a man knocked out someone's eye, or broke someone's arm, precisely the same was to be done to him. If a house collapsed and killed the buyer of the house, the builder had to die. A man who hit his father had his hands cut off; a doctor whose patient died as the result of an operation had his fingers cut off. Robbery, burglary, kidnapping, hiding a runaway slave, and cowardice before the enemy were all punishable by death. The first law of the code read: "If a man bring an accusation against a man, and charge him with a (capital) crime, but cannot prove it, the accuser shall be put to death."

Gradually such punishments as these were replaced by payment of damages; a payment of money was permitted as a substitute for physical revenge, and later the fine became the only punishment. To maintain unity within early societies, the chief would use his influence or power to have the revengeful family content itself with gold rather than blood. The penalty varied with the rank of the offender and the victim. Thus the penalty for knocking out the eye of a common man was sixty shekels of silver (about $300), but for that of a slave only thirty ($150). A plebian who struck another plebian was fined ten shekels ($50), but if he struck an aristocrat it cost him sixty ($300).

AUTHORITY SOLIDIFIES

As time passed, supreme authority became vested in a king or priest, and all pronouncements were backed by the power of the State or the power of the gods. Taboo and myth became crystallized into formal religion and were expressed, in some places, as written law. Powerful economic interests of the time supported the gods and the king, and were favored in return. Crime now came to be viewed as any affront to the gods or the god-image, the king. The handling of crime was taken over by religious and kingly powers.

Gradually courts were formed. The elders, the king, or the priests sat in judgment to settle the conflicts of their people. These courts were not always seats of judgment; many times they were simply a place before which two disputants could present their case. The judge or presiding official would then try to find some way of settling the dispute in a manner satisfactory to both sides. For example, if two neighbors desired part of a piece of land but could not agree on how it was to be divided between them, they could place the matter before such a court. The judge, after hearing both sides, would make the decision. Neither neighbor would get all the property, but each would get something. Among many peoples, however, the use of courts remained optional for several centuries. Often when the offended person was not satisfied with the decision given by the court, he could still seek personal revenge.

CHRISTIANITY INTENSIFIES PUNISHMENT

With the rise of Christianity, however, a subtle change began to occur. The area of what was considered "criminal" began to be extended. Up to now, the *act* (the actual doing or not doing of something) was "criminal." Now the Church assumed control over the *inner* life of man. Certain beliefs and attitudes were considered "wrong," and subjective "crimes"—guilt, fear, apprehension—appeared. People were viewed as behaving criminally—robbing, murdering, uttering heresy—because they were possessed, or occupied by evil spirits doing the bidding of the devil. The task of these spirits or demons was to capture as many souls as possible.

Such a view led to the idea that very harsh punishment was necessary in order to drive out these spirits. Trial by ordeal became common. An accused might submit to having spears thrown at him by his accusers; if none hit him, he was declared innocent. He might be asked to choose between two bowls of food, one poisoned, the other non-poisoned. If he lived after eating from one of the bowls, the matter was considered closed. The ordeal of Peter Bartholomew, accused of lying in the 12th Century, was described as follows:

The fire burned high, and heat filled the air . . . Peter Bartholomew, clad only in his tunic . . . called upon God to witness that . . . if he had lied he would perish in the fire . . . he went into the fire manfully and without fear.

In the midst of it, Bartholomew delayed an instant, and then he passed through safely. When he emerged from the fire, his shirt was not burned.[1]

Since Peter emerged from this "ordeal by fire" unharmed, he was judged innocent of the charge against him.

THE ENLIGHTENMENT

It was not until much later that a concern with the *causes* of crime began to appear. Such a concern came with the overall awakening which occurred during the 18th Century. The growth of scientific thought led to a searching for causes in all areas of knowledge. Protestantism challenged the supremacy of the Church. Skeptics like Montesquieu and Voltaire began to use their minds in an inquiring fashion, ripping apart the veil of superstition and mystery which previously had prevailed over many areas. In 1767, Cesare di Beccaria published *On Crime and Punishment,* and it was then that criminology—the serious and formal study of crime and criminals—was born.

Since individuals have Free Will (the freedom to choose to do right or wrong), he argued, they deserve to be punished if they commit a crime. He emphasized, however, that people who committed the same crimes should be punished by the same penalties. He also argued that crimes and their punishments should be arranged in order of severity, thereby making punishment arbitrary and invariable.

Attempts to explain crime and account for it went hand in hand with the discovery and application of new tools and methods of research. Some individuals became obsessed with the shape and contour of the body, and they began to look for certain identifying physical characteristics which all criminals would possess. Others began to view degeneracy and insanity as causes for crime. The development of applied statistics led to an attempt to show the relation between crime and social phenomena, with some investigators, using quantitative measurements, indicating co-variables such as the rise of crimes of passion in Southern climates during hot weather and the increase of crimes against property in Northern climates during cold weather.

A mid-19th Century prison doctor, Cesare Lombroso, drew on the above to formulate the thesis that criminals engaged in crime not because

---

[1] Ralph O. West, ed., *The Human Side of World History,* Boston, Mass.: Ginn & Co., 1963.

they wanted to but because of inborn tendencies. Others argued that crimes were a product of social conditions. Some psychologists, especially Freud and his followers, traced all aberrative behavior, including crime, to the influences of early life. They argued that faulty development and the interaction of personality factors during the childhood years brought about internal conflicts which generated criminal behavior.

In most parts of the world today, crimes are considered to be those actions dangerous enough to the society's welfare that they are prohibited by law or by custom. All societies prohibit some actions, although what these actions are may vary considerably from society to society. In some primitive societies, for example, certain words and names are considered to be taboo, never to be pronounced. Women in some tribes will not marry a man unless he has killed someone first. At one time, Eskimo sons were expected to kill their parents when they became old and useless and could not provide for themselves.

The Question of Punishment

⌊There are always some people, in any society, who refuse to act in accordance with those customs which the society considers fitting and proper.⌉ There are always some who do not obey the laws.

How should we deal with individuals who break society's laws? What is considered fitting and proper punishment for crime also varies from time to time and from society to society.

In ancient Egypt, beating with a rod was frequent punishment, and mutilation by cutting off nose, ears, hand, or tongue was not uncommon. Under Roman law the emphasis was on severe punishments such as branding, mutilation, or banishment from the society.

With the coming of Christianity, it was felt that criminals should not be punished before they repented their criminal act. Strangely enough, torture was often used to bring about such repentance. In 12th Century London, brutality was common. The death penalty was imposed for such relatively minor crimes as cutting down young trees or petty theft. Other minor crimes were punished by whipping, burning a hole in the ears, cutting out the tongue, or placing individuals in a pillory. When John Stubbs, a Puritan lawyer, wrote a pamphlet criticizing Queen Elizabeth's proposed marriage, his right hand was cut off by order of a judge. Holding up the bleeding stump and raising his hat with his left hand, he cried, "Long live the Queen!"

Today many people the world over say that the practice of *capital punishment* is a carry-over from these earlier brutalities. Capital punishment means that the punishment prescribed for certain crimes is execution—either by hanging, the gas chamber, or the electric chair.

Should individuals who commit very serious crimes be executed by society? A bitter argument rages throughout the world on this question, which we will consider in detail in Chapter 6.

The argument over capital punishment reflects a basic difference in viewpoint over how to treat criminals in general. Should we build more jails? Should we hire more police? Impose longer sentences? Do we need even harsher punishments? Or, should we build more rehabilitation institutions such as work camps, farms, and hospitals where criminals can be given psychological help, medical treatment, and vocational guidance? Should we hire more psychologists and psychiatrists to analyze criminal behavior? Is more lenient treatment needed? More stringent?

What Do You Think?

1. How would you define "crime" at this point?
2. Has the meaning of crime and criminal behavior changed over the years? Explain.

What Is the
Nature of Crime?

3

What do we mean by crime and criminal behavior? Are there different types of criminals? Do different categories of crime exist? In this chapter, you will read about four different kinds of crime—ordinary, professional, organized, and white-collar. In what ways are these categories different? In what ways are they similar? Can you think of other categories which you could add to these?

1. THE ORDINARY CRIMINAL *

Our first glimpse of crime and criminals takes place in a municipal courts building in a typical city.

The criminal is twenty-five years old, somewhat chubby, of average height, and rather "worn-down" looking. He has been in and out of prisons continually since he was nineteen. He is a small-time burglar who has received nothing but two prison terms for his efforts. This is his third arrest for burglary. He pleads guilty.

The Judge states that he will be sentenced to five more years in the penitentiary. "Five years!" the man exclaims. Then he is crying. The Judge says that he is sorry, but that there is nothing he can do. It is the law.

An elderly man enters. He is forty-nine and has been arrested for drunken driving. In searching his car, the police found a concealed weapon for which the man had no permit. He has been arrested before for drunken-

---

* Reprinted from David Dressler, *Parole Chief.* New York, N. Y.: The Viking Press, 1951. Copyright © 1951 Viking Press. Reprinted by permission of the author and his agent, James Brown Associates, Inc.

ness and disturbing the peace, but never jailed. He is a steady worker and tells this to the judge; he has held the same job for over twenty years. Why did he have that weapon? He mumbles that he was taking it to a friend and didn't know it was in the car. He is given thirty days in the county jail, but the sentence is suspended, and he goes free on probation and a promise of good behavior in the future.

The Juvenile Court is a place of heartbreak. A mother agrees that she cannot control her son. "He isn't a bad boy, your Honor," she tells the judge, "only wild." He must go away to reform school. Repeatedly he has stolen tires from cars; sometimes the cars themselves. He is only fourteen.

Now it is the criminal court. A slack-jawed, bearded youth has been arrested and accused of stealing a sweater from a shop in a rundown section of town. He has had numerous convictions for petty theft. The judge asks: "Did you threaten to kill this man?" indicating the shop owner, an older, somewhat stooped man with glasses. "I didn't have no weapon," says the youth.

Now another youth enters the court, accompanied by his father. The boy has had his seventh run-in with the police. He is eighteen, husky, and combs his hair continually. He is a "good boy," says his father. But he and a number of his buddies get high on beer one night. He gets into an argument with one of his friends and beats him severely. He is on parole from a previous conviction for assault; he attacked one of his schoolmates with a broken bottle. "The police see us standing around the neighborhood and pick us up," he says. "There ain't nothing to do where us guys live." He dropped out of high school after two years: "I just never dug school." He had a job as an apprentice butcher, but was fired after his conviction. "What do you want to do with your life?" asks the judge. "I don't know," answers the boy.

Three Mexican boys are on trial in a Circuit Court for attempted burglary. They had tried to hold up a laundry, but were apprehended by a policeman passing by. They have enough money to hire a lawyer. They appear in court clean, and looking very neat. The defense attorney is a Negro who is very talented. The jury, unconvinced by the policeman's testimony, returns a verdict of Not Guilty.

What Do You Think?

What crime have each of these individuals committed? Why are each of these acts considered to be a crime?

2. MAXIE THE GONIFF—A PROFESSIONAL THIEF *

*Next, we take a look at a professional thief. In what ways does he dif-
fer from the individuals described in the previous reading?*

Maxie the Goniff is a professional. He is not very bright. His body
is slight and springy; his fingers are long, tapering, and nervous. His face
resembles a parrot's, the beak long and hooked downward. His eyes are
furtive. He decided over fifty years ago that picking "pokes" was a fine
way of making a living. He apprenticed himself to a master, studied hard,
graduated with honors, and went on his own. He wouldn't tell me how
old he was at the time we spoke, but my guess is that he was at least
sixty-five. . . .

Like most of his kind, Maxie has a long criminal record. He has been
arrested seventy-one times in twenty-two states.

"Doesn't speak so well for you, Maxie," I goaded him. . . .

He flushed angrily. "Every one of them pinches came after a whole
season's work. In fifty years I done six years time. I'm living good—well,
pretty good—for forty-four years and it cost me six years! You should have
it so good!"

He claims that both his parents were alcoholics, that they put him
out of the house when he was twelve, and that he has been on his own
ever since. For a time he was a petty thief, then a shoplifter, and finally,
while still a kid, he met a man who took him on as an apprentice dip and
taught him the business.

Picking pockets *is* a business, Maxie insists. "You've got to figure
a certain amount of risk in any business. Suppose I open a saloon, I'm
taking a chance, no? I might go broke, I might have to pay too much protection—it's all business."

Like all commercial enterprises, Maxie's has its seasons. "Summers
we work the resorts, like Coney Island and the buses and subways going
to and from. Beaches are good too. Certain holidays is season for us.
Before Easter and Christmas. There's lots of shopping. That's when I
hit department stores. In the elevators or even on the floor."

When he has had a run of bad luck he will depart from his more
accustomed beat and cover a church wedding. "You don't often find much
dough on the guys, but brother! are they easy to take! They don't expect
a thief in a church."

Occasional gravy is a convention or parade. Maxie plays the crowds.

---

* Reprinted from David Dressler, *Parole Chief.* © Copyright 1951 Viking Press.
Reprinted by permission of the author and his agent, James Brown Associates, Inc.

He loves American Legion groups because "half the time they don't even know *the next morning* whether they've been hooked or just spent the dough!"

Maxie takes pride in his technique. He has little use for the lone operator, although he admits there are some good ones. He considers they take too many risks. . . .

He likes to work in a mob of two or four people. Say you're on a subway or elevator. "You pick your mark and try to figure where he keeps his wallet. It ain't hard to find out. You just jostle the sucker and move off. Right away he puts his hand where he's got the wallet to see if it's there. He tips you off.

"Of course, if he don't fall for that, you've got to *fan* him. You feel around, very easy, until you locate the poke.

"Then comes pratting. You prat the guy around. That means you push him around, edge him around, not hard, gentle, just enough to distract his attention. Also to get him into position, the position you want him in for the score."

The man who does the pushing is the "stall." When the victim is in position, the "duke" (hand) of one thief extracts the poke. This man is called, variously, a "hook," "tool," "wire," or "instrument." He is the most skillful member of the team. The victim's attention is directed to the stall as the hook takes the wallet. Maxie is a hook.

"Funny thing," he said, chuckling. "Some guys look for a poke in a hip pocket. They like to take it from there. I'd rather score out of the breast pocket. Why? Because the sucker thinks he's cute, see? . . . He thinks if he carries it in the breast pocket it's tough to take. It is, but a good thief likes that kind of meat. I always do." (I doubt it. Professional thieves are awful liars. Chances are, Maxie, good businessman that he is, will always go for the easier score when possible.)

While taking from the inside pocket, the wire "shades" the duke—covers his hand so the victim won't see it, perhaps with a newspaper. "What I do," says Maxie, "is 'put a throw' in his face. I shade my duke with a paper and annoy the guy by flappin' it under his nose. That makes 'im mad. He's concentratin' on the throw while I'm 'takin' off the score.'

"In a good crowd, on a hip job, the 'push grift' works. No shadin' the duke, nothin'. Everybody's pushing, so you push all you want, and the guy don't even see or feel your hand."

In digging for the wallet the "straight hoist" is commonly employed. The thief puts the first two fingers, held stiffly, into the pocket. He stiffens his body, lifts up on his toes, and out comes the wallet.

The next step is "cleaning." "The stall distracts attention, say. Now the wire's got the poke. He has to get clean right away. . . . If the sucker 'blows' (discovers his loss) he's gonna figure right away it's the wire, because the wire was closest to him. So I pass the wallet on right away to one of my stalls—the one who will be first off the car or elevator. If the guy grabs me I'm clean. I beef like hell. If he goes for the stall, he drops the poke and he's clean. Or better yet, he plants it on some bystander and we take it back later."

Maxie is proudest of the fact that he is a specialist among specialists, "a left-breach hook." That's a man who can draw a score out of a left pants pocket. "There ain't many can do that. It's hard. Try it!"

I asked him how much he earned a year by grifting. He became very evasive, even apologetic. "Oh, I had my ups and downs. Why talk about it? You do all right, year in, year out, if you're good. Some years I run five, ten thousand. Other times not so good. . . ."

"Where did your money go? . . ."

"Well, the horses got a lot of it. Craps. Cards. Women. And I had to eat too." He forgot to mention that he has a wife and two children who are dependent upon him for their support.

I have never known an affluent pickpocket. I don't believe they make as much as Maxie claims, and their money seems to go fast. They live riotously. Some are drug addicts at times in their lives. Many have wives and children. I've never known one who wasn't a confirmed gambler or who wasn't fresh out of money every time I inquired.

Maxie is hurt because thieves are generally regarded with contempt, even in the professional underworld. He doesn't like to admit that contempt is earned. But the average dip is penny ante. Moreover, he is weak-willed, often turns in a pal to save his own skin. Perhaps because he is a weakling, the pickpocket is often a stool pigeon.

Maxie insists there is honor among thieves in his game. "Sure, a guy rats now and then. That don't prove nothin'. You'll always find a few rats. But most of us stick together. We help each other. We put up fall dough for a guy in trouble."

"Did you ever rat, Maxie?"

"Like I say, we stick together. We put up fall dough." . . .

"Maxie," I asked, "if you had it to do over again, what would you be instead of a pickpocket?"

"What's wrong," he snapped, "with this racket?"

What Do You Think?

1. How would you describe Maxie? Why?
2. How would you explain the fact that Maxie's opinion of himself does not agree with that of the author?
3. At the end of the article, Maxie asks "What's wrong with this racket?" How would you answer him?

3.   ORGANIZED CRIME—HOW THE MOB CONTROLS CHICAGO *

Now we take a look at organized crime. Could this exist in your city?

"Chicago," a highly placed U.S. law enforcement official said in a recent interview, "is a city in the grip of the mob. It is worse in this respect than any other American community. The Syndicate is so solidly entrenched there and is so monolithic in structure that it is almost impossible to root out. It has worked its way into nearly every facet of the life of the city."

Like all major American cities, Chicago faces other staggering difficulties—among them, deteriorating race relations and a shocking need for urban rehabilitation. It has also made progress in many fields, but the mark of the Syndicate is on the city and its environs, and that brand, which affects all the city's other problems, makes Chicago's blight unique in the United States, if not in the world.

You cannot go into a restaurant in Chicago or its suburbs in Cook County—730 square miles with nearly 2,000,000 people, outside the city limits—and be sure that you are not eating Syndicate beef, drinking Syndicate beer and whiskey, using a tablecloth and napkin supplied by a Syndicate linen service, parking your car and checking your hat with Syndicate-owned concessions, even drinking out of glasses cleansed by a Syndicate-owned sterilizing machine. In so doing, you are paying money into a vast two-billion-dollar-a-year industry—estimated by Cook County's Sheriff Richard Ogilvie to be Chicago's biggest, by far—and your dollars are being used to finance such other underworld activities as narcotics, prostitution, extortion, political corruption, usury, mayhem and murder. In many instances, you have no choice. If the restaurant is not owned outright by the Syndicate, through some front man, the chances are that the restaurateur has been forced to accept Syndicate supplies and services through judicious use of muscle—which in simple language is, "You buy from us, Mac, or else." The files of the Justice Department's Organized Crime Unit in Chicago are filled with such cases. The victims sometimes complain, but they never have the courage to testify.

Moreover, in Chicago—as in no other American city—you may be doing business with the Syndicate when you subscribe to a diaper service, hire a scavenging firm to haul your garbage away, buy a neon sign, park your car in a downtown garage, purchase bread in a supermarket, order a carpet, contract for plumbing work, get airline tickets through a travel

---

* Bill Davidson, "How The Mob Controls Chicago," *The Saturday Evening Post,* November 9, 1963. © 1963 The Curtis Publishing Company.

agency, take out a loan at a bank or even go to the polls to vote. Since the days of Al Capone, the Syndicate has had a strong voice in the selection of aldermen from Chicago's First Ward—the city's wealthiest, since it comprises the Loop, the financial district and all of the city's great department stores and downtown theaters and hotels. One of Chicago's State Senators is . . . a nephew by marriage of the ex-convict boss of bosses of the Chicago Syndicate. . . .

THE WIDE-OPEN SUBURBS

Attempts to dispute the mob's control are discouraged. Not long ago a schoolteacher . . . led a civic meeting in Stone Park, a suburb of Chicago, to protest faulty town services, such as the water supply. After the meeting he was approached by . . . the Syndicate boss of vice and gambling in the so-called Mannheim Strip, near Chicago's O'Hare Airport, who roared "Don't you know who runs this town?" He then proceeded to beat the teacher unmercifully, in full view of several witnesses, including at least two policemen. Nothing ever happened to him. The chief of police of Stone Park is the gambling boss's cousin.

In wide-open Cicero, Syndicate headquarters town in the Capone days, detectives from the office of the State's Attorney recently raided the rat's nest of bookie joints, bordellos, B-girl taverns and strip-tease emporiums. The Cicero police offered no help. On the contrary, when the detectives returned to their cars, they found all of them tagged for illegal parking.

Last year in the town of Oak Park two crack cops from Chicago's incorruptible Intelligence Division trailed a Syndicate car into an alley. Out jumped Sam (Teetz) Battaglia, one of Giancana's top *Cosa Nostra* aides in western Cook County, and Battaglia's bodyguard, Rocco Salvatore. Zitek and Nash flashed their badges, whereupon the hoodlums began to throw punches. It was an uneven battle. Zitek is a tough Navy veteran and Nash a former Golden Gloves boxer. Salvatore was soon flattened and Battaglia, suspected by Chicago police to be one of the Syndicate's most feared "hit men"—the mob name for gangland killers—was on his knees, pleading, "Don't hit me no more! Don't hit me no more!" when Oak Park police arrived. But instead of taking Battaglia and his companion into custody, the local cops arrested the two Chicago policemen—even though they also held commissions as Cook County deputy sheriffs.

A few weeks ago I personally became aware of the power of the Chicago's *Cosa Nostra* when I drove through the suburb of Oak Park with Detective Zitek and a federal law enforcement officer. As we cruised past Syndicate chief Giancana's lavish yellow brick home, we were intercepted by an Oak Park squad car. The cop in the squad car made us identify ourselves. Then, though we had arrived in the area just seconds before, he said, "I got a call on you guys from headquarters." Immediately thereafter we were picked up by a tail which followed us until we returned to Chicago. It was a black Oldsmobile from one of the Syndicate-controlled auto agencies. "Sometimes," Zitek said, "I think their communications system is faster than ours."

In Chicago itself the story is equally sordid. The city's Press Club is in a Syndicate-frequented hotel, the St. Clair. Nearby, just a few blocks from the swank Near North Side residential area, are three other hotels—the Berkshire, the Devonshire, and the Maryland—which swarm with Syndicate pimps and prostitutes, according to the Intelligence Division of the Chicago Police Department. These hotels are the core of the fiefdom of Jimmy Allegretti, who is in charge of vice and narcotics in the Near North Side for the Syndicate. Despite frequent raids by carefully chosen police-men, and despite the fact that Allegretti has been convicted of conspiracy to hijack whiskey for inexpensive distribution to his hotels and restaurants (he is out of jail on appeal), his operations continue. "The *honest* cops," says a cynical Chicago newspaperman, "can't be everywhere. We'll have this plague in the heart of downtown Chicago as long as there's clout and the police haven't cleaned out all of the kinky cops." (In Chicago's unique vernacular, "clout" is political influence through payoffs and otherwise; "kinky" means crooked, corrupt, in the pay of the mob.)

On State Street, renowned in Chicago song and poesy as "that great street," there are a dozen B-girl and strip joints—with all attendant divertissements for the tired conventioneer—within sight of both Police Headquarters and the famous Loop department stores. These are the personal domain of Gus Alex, one of Giancana's executive officers in the Syndicate. In one joint, the Star and Garter Lounge, across the street from staid Sears Roebuck's national headquarters, I posed as an electrical equip-ment salesman attending a convention at the Conrad Hilton Hotel and was offered, in quick succession, a chance to buy a $2.50 drink for a B-girl, a narcotics "fix," a female companion to grace my hotel room, an op-portunity to place a bet on a Florida horse race the following day, and a ride to a gambling hideaway in Cicero where I could satisfy my lust for "action."

A mile or so from this seamy but profitable Gus Alex enterprise is the more plush Rush Street complex of high clubs, bars and restaurants —all part of Jimmy Allegretti's territory. In the heart of Rush Street is a bustling establishment called The Living Room, formerly known as The Trade Winds. At that time it was patronized by all the top Syndicate members and by nearly every celebrity passing through Chicago, from Elizabeth Taylor to the ubiquitous Frank Sinatra. The owner of record of The Trade Winds was a man named Arthur Adler. On January 20, 1960, Adler left his office to meet his wife for dinner, and disappeared. Two months later a sewer inspector lifted a manhole cover on a sedate residential street and discovered a nude, decomposed body without a mark of violence on it. The body was identified as that of Adler.

The Intelligence Division of the Chicago Police Department has two theories about the demise of Adler. The first holds that Adler went into hock to the Mob when he opened The Trade Winds and a second night club, The Black Onyx. He accepted complete Mob control as to who his suppliers would be, and he paid the standard Syndicate shylocking rates of 240 per cent a year. According to this theory, Adler had not only fallen behind in his payments but had indicated he might tell the story of his troubles to a special federal grand jury, which had subpoenaed him.

The second theory—a much simpler one—is that the Syndicate had asked Adler to fence some jewels which one of its members had stolen from a suite in one of Chicago's luxury hotels—and Adler, beset by what police believe was a $63,000 debt to the mob, had held out some of the money for himself. In any event, the otherwise-respected businessman ended up very much dead.

The Cook County coroner issued a verdict that death was caused "by strangling by hand or instrument," but Chicago police have information that Adler was killed by a much more ingenious method. They say that the nightclub owner was taken to the cold-storage room of one of the Syndicate's meat wholesaling plants—the same one in which, *Cosa Nostra* dignitaries have bragged, a gangster was once ground up and distributed to the city's restaurants as Manburgers. Adler, according to the police, was tortured for a while. Then the business end of a fire extinguisher was inserted in each of his ears. The fire extinguishers were turned on and the tremendous pressure of carbon dioxide gas caused massive brain hemorrhage and seemingly natural death. If the routine sewer inspection had not occurred, Adler's body would have been washed away by the spring freshets.

Adler became Chicago's 941st unsolved gangland murder victim since 1919. According to the Chicago Crime Commission's files, there have now been nearly 1,000 such professional slayings—an average of nearly 23 per year. This is a record unequaled anywhere else in the United States. Yet the sickness of respectable, hardworking, enterprising Chicago—part of its inferiority complex about being the Second City to New York—is its refusal to admit to itself that murder and organized lawlessness and an all-powerful Syndicate are crucial facts of life in the community. "Sometimes the people in Chicago remind me of the Germans during the Hitler period," Chief of Sheriff's Police Arthur Bilek told me. "You tell them that a Buchenwald is in their midst and they say it's impossible, nothing but outsiders' propaganda." Capt. William Duffy, director of the Chicago Police Department's Intelligence Division, says, "Our biggest obstacle is the refusal of the public even to accept the *fact* that organized crime exists here." Frank Kiernan, chief of the Justice Department's Organized Crime Unit in Chicago, laments, "To the people of this city, it's like a football game—the Cops versus the Mob. They sit in the grandstand, sometimes rooting for one side, sometimes for the other—and they don't realize *they* are right down there in the middle of the action with the players."

This attitude exists on all levels of society in Chicago and its suburbs. At parties people would say to me, "Now don't you be like those other Eastern writers and slander us again with all that phony 1930's gangster stuff. Why don't you write about our parks and our new Greenwich Village in the Old Town section of the city?" They made jokes about the Syndicate, as if it were composed of bumbling, lovable Damon Runyon characters, and I found that certain mobsters, like Milwaukee Phil Alderisio and Frank (Strongy) Ferraro, had fans who followed all their exploits in the papers the way they read about such Chicago sports figures as Ernie Banks and George Halas.

One of the city's leading newspaper editors warned me, "Don't make the mistake of emphasizing organized crime here. It's nowhere near as bad as it was fifteen years ago." When I protested that none of the law-enforcement officials agreed with him, he said, "Let me call in my top crime reporter. He'll tell you." The reporter was summoned, and the editor put the question to him. "As *bad* as it was fifteen years ago?" the reporter exclaimed. "Why it's ten times worse!" A crime reporter on another newspaper was even more blunt. "There are two governments in Chicago," he said. "The first is elected by the people. The second government is the Syndicate. Sometimes it's hard to say which one runs the city."

What Do You Think?

1. What evidence does the author offer in support of his statement that "the Syndicate is so solidly entrenched (in Chicago) . . . that it is almost impossible to root it out"?

2. Captain Duffy, the director of Chicago's Police Intelligence Division, stated that "our biggest obstacle is the refusal of the public even to accept the fact that organized crime exists here." If this is so, why might Chicagoans be unwilling to admit this?

4. THE WHITE COLLAR CROOK *

Lastly, a view of what is often described as "white collar crime." Do the individuals described here seem familiar?

A graduate student in an urban university, in order to supplement his income, took a job as an extra salesman in a shoe store on Saturdays and other rush days. He had no previous experiences as a shoe salesman or in any other regular business. He described his experience in this store thus:

"One day I was standing in the front part of the store, waiting for the next customer. A man came in and asked if we had any high, tan shoes. I told him that we had no shoes of that style. He thanked me and walked out of the store. The floorwalker came up to me and asked me what the man wanted. I told him what the man asked for and what I replied. The floorwalker said angrily: 'Damn it! We're not here to sell what they want. We're here to sell what we've got.' He went on to instruct me that when a customer came into the store, the first thing to do was to get him to sit down and take off his shoe so that he couldn't get out of the store. 'If we don't have what he wants,' he said, 'bring him something else and try to interest him in that style. If he is still uninterested, inform the floorwalker and he will send one of the regular salesmen, and if that doesn't work, a third salesman will be sent to him. Our policy is that no customer gets out of the store without a sale until at least three salesmen have worked on him. By that time he feels that he must be a crank and will generally buy something whether he wants it or not.

"I learned from other clerks that if a customer needed a 7-B shoe and we did not have that size in the style he desired, I should try on an 8-A or 7-C or some other size. The sizes were marked in code so that the customer did not know what the size was, and it might be necessary to lie to him about the size; also his foot might be injured by the misfit. But the rule was to sell him a pair of shoes, preferably a pair that fit but some other pair if necessary.

"I learned also that the clerks received an extra commission if they sold the out-of-style shoes left over from earlier seasons, which were called 'spiffs.' The regular salesmen made a practice of selling spiffs to anyone who appeared gullible and generally had to claim either that this was the latest style or that it had been the style earlier and was coming

* From Edwin H. Sutherland, *White Collar Crime.* Copyright 1949 by Holt, Rinehart and Winston, Inc. Reprinted by permission of Holt, Rinehart and Winston.

back this season, or that it was an old style but much better quality than present styles. The clerk had to size up the customer and determine which one of these lies would be most likely to result in a sale.

"Several years later I became acquainted with a man who worked for several years as a regular salesman in shoe stores in Seattle. When I described to him the methods I had learned in the shoe store where I worked, he said: 'Every shoe store in Seattle except one does exactly the same things and I learned to be a shoe salesman in exactly the same manner you did.' "

Another young man who was holding his first position as a shoe salesman in a small city wrote an autobiographical statement in which he included the following instructions given him by the manager of the shoe store:

"My job is to move out shoes and I hire you to assist in this. I am perfectly glad to fit a person with a pair of shoes if we have his size, but I am willing to misfit him if it is necessary in order to sell him a pair of shoes. I expect you to do the same. If you do not like this, someone else can have your job. While you are working for me, I expect you to have no scruples about how you sell shoes."

A man who had been a school teacher and had never been officially involved in any delinquencies secured a position as agent of a book-publishing company and was assigned to public school work. He soon learned that the publishing company bribed the members of the textbook committee in order to secure adoptions of their books. With considerable shame he began to use this method of bribery because he felt it was necessary in order to make a good record. Partly because he disliked this procedure but principally because this work kept him away from home much of the time, he decided that he would become a lawyer. He moved to a large city, registered for night courses in a law school, and secured a daytime job as a claim agent for a casualty insurance company. About two years later he was convicted of embezzling the funds of the insurance company. A portion of his autobiography describes the process by which he got into this difficulty:

"Almost immediately after I got into this business I learned two things: first, the agents who got ahead with the company were the ones who made settlements at low figures and without taking cases into court; second, the settlements were generally made by collusion with the lawyers and doctors for the claimants. Most of the lawyers for the claimants were ambulance-chasers and were willing to make settlements because they got their fees without any work. The claim agent for the insurance company got a secret kick-back out of the settlement. When I learned this was the way to get ahead in the casualty insurance business, I went in for it in a big way. Accidentally I left some papers loose in my office, from which it was discovered that I was 'knocking down' on the settlements. The insurance company accused me of taking money which belonged to them, but actually I was taking money which belonged to the claimants."

The following statement was made by a young man who had graduated from a recognized school of business, had become a certified public accountant, and had been employed for several years in a respected firm of public accountants in a large city.

"While I was a student in the school of business I learned the principles of accounting. After I had worked for a time for an accounting firm I found I had failed to learn many important things about accounting. An accounting firm gets its work from business firms and, within limits, must make the reports which those business firms desire. The accounting firm for which I work is respected and there is none better in the city. On my first assignment I discovered some irregularities in the books of the firm and these would lead anyone to question the financial policies of that firm. When I showed my report to the manager of our accounting firm, he said that was not a part of my assignment and I should leave it out. Although I was confident that the business firm was dishonest, I had to conceal this information. Again and again I have been compelled to do the same thing in other assignments. I got so disgusted with things of this sort that I wish I could leave the profession. I guess I must stick to it, for it is the only occupation for which I have training."

*　　*　　*　　*　　*

A chemist who had been employed to advise a firm as to the scientific basis for claims in advertisements made the following statement regarding his experiences:

"When I got members of the firm off in a corner and we were talking confidentially, they frankly deplored the misrepresentations in their advertisements. At the same time they said it was necessary to advertise in this manner in order to attract the attention of customers and sell their products. Since other firms are making extravagant claims regarding their products, we must make extravagant claims regarding our products. A mere statement of fact regarding our products would make no impression on customers in the face of the ads of other firms.

"One of the important automobile companies began to advertise the interest rate on the unpaid balance in installment purchases as six per cent, when in fact the rate was more than eleven per cent. Within a few weeks the other automobile companies began to advertise their interest rates as six per cent, although their actual rates, also, were more than eleven per cent. Again, when one automobile company published an advertisement of the price and specification of a certain car, together with a picture of a more expensive model, thus misrepresenting its cars, the other companies in the industry generally published similar advertisements with similar misrepresentation. Within a few months after the tire dealers had solemnly adopted a code of ethics in advertising, including a pledge not to use misrepresentations, one tire manufacturer announced a special cut-rate price for tires on the Fourth of July, in which the savings were grossly misrepresented; several other tire manufacturers promptly made similar announcements of cut-rate sales with similar misrepresentations. Thus competition in advertising drives the participants to the extreme, and when one corporation violates the law in this respect the other corporations do the same."

What Do You Think?

1. Do the individuals described in this reading have anything in common? Explain.

2. After considering the examples presented in this reading, how would you define "white collar" crime?

ACTIVITIES FOR INVOLVEMENT

1. In "How the Mob Controls Chicago," Bill Davidson referred to the fact that many people refused to admit that organized crime even existed in Chicago. Might this tendency not to admit the existence of unpleasant facts carry over into other areas? Form a committee of from four to six class members to draw up a list of some of the most pressing problems (in addition to crime) currently facing American society (for example, slums, racial discrimination, alienation of youth, poverty, etc.), and interview a sample of your community. What percentage of those interviewed feel that such problems exist in your community?

2. Invite a lawyer to speak to your class on the topic "Equality Before the Law." Some people have remarked that all people are equal before the law, but that some are more equal than others. What do you think this means? Would you agree or not? Ask the lawyer to comment on the statement.

3. Compare the similarities and differences which exist among the individuals in each of the readings in this chapter. In what ways are they similar? In what ways are they different? How would you explain these similarities and differences?

4. Recall the instructions given by the manager of the shoe store to the young man holding his first position as a shoe salesman. Suppose you are that salesman. There are a number of ways in which you might have

reacted (out loud or to yourself). Pick the position which is closest to the one you would take:

    a. Business is business. It is up to the customer to be on his guard and to know what he wants and needs. Anyone stupid enough to let himself be sold a pair of shoes that doesn't fit deserves what he gets.

    b. What you suggest is utterly dishonest. I'll look elsewhere for a job.

    c. I don't agree, but it won't help matters much to protest right now. I'll take the job, do my best to fit my customers as accurately as I can, and then try to change the store's policy later when I get into a position of responsibility.

    d. I don't like it, but what can I do? If I don't take the job, someone else will. And then where will I be? Idealistic, maybe, but I still won't have a job.

What other replies to the owner might you offer? Defend your choice.

    5.   The National Opinion Research Center (NORC) of the University of Chicago, in trying to get an idea of the amount of crime that exists, surveyed 10,000 households, asking whether the person questioned, or any member of his or her household, had been a victim of crime during 1965–1966. The results were then compared with the national statistics compiled by the Federal Bureau of Investigation and published annually as a part of its report, "Crime in the United States, Uniform Crime Reports (UCR). (The UCR are based on citizen complaints or independent police discovery and are collected from local police officials.) This comparison is shown in the table below:

UCR AND NORC SURVEY INDEX CRIME RATES COMPARED, BY REGION, 1965

(Rates per 100,000 population)

CRIMES	NORTHEAST		NORTH CENTRAL		SOUTH		WEST	
	NORC	UCR	NORC	UCR	NORC	UCR	NORC	UCR
Willful homicide	3	3.6	0	3.7	10	8.0	0	4.2
Forcible rape	25	8.5	42	11.8	48	10.8	57	17.2
Robbery [1]	139	49.9	85	76.6	48	45.6	133	81.9
Aggravated assault	164	84.7	233	84.1	173	140.6	361	113.5
Burglary [1]	746	515.9	987	523.5	866	552.4	1,348	1,078.5
Larceny ($50 and over) [1] ..	480	392.6	594	325.4	596	332.4	855	622.2
Motor vehicle theft [1]	278	285.8	170	244.5	96	175.7	380	351.5
Against the person	328	146.7	360	176.2	279	205.0	551	216.8
Against property	1,504	1,194.3	1,751	1,093.4	1,558	1,060.5	2,583	2,052.2

[1] NORC figures are for individuals only; UCR figures are not adjusted and reflect all offenses known to the police, not just those for individuals.
Source: "UCR, 1965," pp. 52–53; NORC survey, p. 21.

    Refer to table. What difference do you notice between the UCR and NORC Survey Index Crime Rates? What does this seem to indicate about the extent of crime reported in the UCR? How would you explain this?

4

What Causes Crime?

What causes crime? Can we determine its source? Though a number of explanations have been offered, none, as yet, has been deemed totally satisfactory. This chapter presents several accounts to illustrate how a variety of people were inducted into criminal behavior.

1. ATTITUDES TOWARD CRIME *

How do people feel about criminals and criminal behavior? How do you feel? Compare your attitudes with those given below.

"When we arrest some hoodlum on a street, and a crowd gathers, and the punk has to be subdued, who do you think the sympathies of the crowd are with?" asks a veteran Boston patrolman. "With the criminal. We get booed. Bystanders tell us to take it easy, though we're handling a hopped-up character with a knife. *We're* the bad guys."

Last year, a Cleveland city councilman was convicted of income-tax evasion and given a suspended federal-prison sentence. Yet last November he was overwhelmingly re-elected by a respectable west-side Cleveland neighborhood, which customarily takes pride in its high moral standards. . . .

"I'd rather my son had prostitutes to go to instead of getting into trouble with my neighbors' daughters," said an advertising man. "After

---

* Excerpted from Samuel Grafton, "The Climate of Crime," *McCall's Magazine,* March 1965. Copyright 1965 *McCall's Magazine.* Reprinted by permission McCall Corporation, Inc.

all, I have to live with my neighbors." A theater usher said: "Let the girls walk the streets. They have their job to do, same as everybody else." "I'm in favor of a red-light district," said a waitress. "Then child-molesters might leave youngsters alone." . . .

A druggist in a small, clean, pretty-as-a-poster town has been holding off on installing a soda fountain, because he is afraid the youngsters, hanging around, "would steal me blind." He finds that juveniles take articles they can't conceivably need or use, "just for kicks." He, too, calls parents to complain of junior larceny. "Sometimes I don't even get a surprised reaction," he says. "They tell me just to put whatever their kids stole on their bill." The local grade-school principal was questioned about the situation. "I don't think it's any worse here than anywhere else," he said mildly. "It's nothing to be alarmed about." The local chamber of commerce ignores the problem. "It doesn't want to give the village a bad name," says a prominent resident, and so its merchant members simply swallow their losses. "If something small is taken, like a candy bar, you don't even call the parents," says a storekeeper. "Why lose a five-hundred-dollar-a-year customer for ten cents?" . . .

A second Cleveland councilman, arrested and convicted a few weeks ago for taking a $5,000 bribe to get a restaurant a liquor license, was quoted as saying, in tones of outrage: "Why, I was just doing the man a favor, trying to help him out. It's done all the time." . . .

"I parked on a downtown street," says a prominent New Yorker, himself a former city official, "and a policeman began to write out a ticket. I noticed there were ten other cars on the block, none ticketed. I asked about them. The policeman told me they were none of my business. I then said to him I wouldn't accept my ticket without a stink unless he ticketed every other car. He looked at me for a long moment and tore my ticket up." . . .

Our attitude toward cheating is another case in point. Cheating is not new, but boasting about it is, and another image of our time is the respectable father of a family boasting about how he did the government in the eye on his latest income-tax return. Often he will tell how clever he was in this regard at the dinner table, before his children. At the social luncheon table, the remark "Let me have the check. I'll put it on the expense account" is almost as common in some circles as "Please pass the butter." . . .

We seem, . . . to seek applause for doing things that are wrong in themselves. At colleges and universities, cheating on exams seems to be the undergraduate equivalent of tax evasion. . . . Several Pennsylvania students felt that such cheating had become an "in" thing to do and conferred status on those who got away with it. It is not enough to cheat; others must know.

A Los Angeles student, queried on how his friends felt about the question of honesty in general, remarked: "They feel there aren't enough free things in the world, so if you can get something for nothing, you'd better snatch at it." He recalled that one girl in his crowd had been found stealing money at house parties; she was told to quit, but that was all. Her invitations continued as before. . . .

Carl D. Dalke, president of the Chicago Better Business Bureau, discussing complaints against some automobile dealers for sharp practices, said: "Ethics is a two-way street. We also get complaints from companies against individuals today, though we don't process them. There are people who will sign a contract with a dealer for a new car, delivery in two weeks or so. The car they show for trade-in has four good tires and a spare; but when they bring the car to turn it in, it has four baldies, no spare, and no jack." . . .

"Everybody's an operator; everybody's a crook," said a Puerto Rican cabdriver. "I'm going to stay honest. That's because I'm a chump. I know it means I'll have to stay poor."

What Do You Think?

1. Summarize the feelings which seem to be expressed in these statements. In what ways are they similar? Different? Explain.
2. The Puerto Rican cabdriver stated that "everybody's a crook." Would you agree? Why? If you would not agree, what evidence could you offer to refute his statement?

2. THE BEGINNINGS OF STREET LIFE *

What follows is a tape-recorded interview between a sociologist investigating delinquent behavior and the leader of a teen-age gang. What factors caused Hank to "hang out" in the streets?

(Q) *How did you first start hanging out, do you remember?*

(A) You wouldn't believe it, but when I was nine, ten, I used to be bashful. I just didn't want to go nowhere. We didn't even have no television then, but I'd just lay around by the radio, listen to that all night. 'Till time to go to bed. Or I'd read. Fiction. True stuff. All them old books, like *Smoke Blows West, Daniel Boone* westerns, stuff like that. Mysteries. Football stories. Baseball stories. Comics once in a while. You couldn't get me out of the house. My ma would say, "For Pete's sake! Why don't you go outside and play?"

---

* Excerpted from "Gang Boy," David Dressler (ed.), *Readings in Criminology and Penology*, New York, N. Y.: Columbia Univ. Press, 1964.

I was about eleven, twelve, when I commenced going out a little. There was these guys I went to school with. We'd ride home together on our bike. One of us would say, "Where you going tonight?" "Where *you* going?" "Well," he'd say, "let's go over and get Johnny. He'll go riding with us." So we'd go get him. There'd be three, four guys that way. There wasn't nothing else to do. You don't want to stay home all the time.

After a while it wasn't just bike riding. We'd maybe go to a show. Or we'd get together some money and go to Ferry's [a concession park], ride the roller coaster.

Hanging out happens gradual. You don't realize you're starting a gang. You feel jittery at home. You don't know what to do with yourself. You know the other guys will be on a certain corner. Or a malt shop. You say, "Hell! I haven't nothing better to do. I'll just walk over and kick it around a little with the fellows." You get so you head for the spot 'most every night.

Then, from hanging around, you commence cutting up now and then. When I was twelve, thirteen, we used to think it was smart to walk past a newsstand and when the guy turned his back we'd snatch a bunch of papers. If he seen us we'd throw them in his face and run. We just did it to be ornery. You did what the others did.

The first thing I ever took to amount to anything was when I was twelve. Me and Sloppy started out to make a night of it. Well, that night seemed awful long, boy, once you got in the middle of it! We didn't have nothing to do. We was kind of sleepy, we wanted to keep going, so naturally, we was going to find something to do.

We was sitting around, and we seen this bicycle parked up on a lawn, right in front. It was a real keen deal, one of them English makes. The guy left it out there where it had no business being, so we jumped on it and took off. Sloppy was driving it. I hung on the back. We hadn't had it no more than a couple of hours, when zooooom! The juvenile officers come around the corner in a car. We tried to get away but we hit some gravel and slid and fell, ass over teakettle. We busted out a couple of spokes. They took us downtown and called our folks to come down. The guy that owned the bike come down, too. He was a grown guy. The cops told him they didn't think we realized how serious it was, what we done, and we didn't, at the time. So they let us go after our folks paid for the damage.

By this time we had quite a few fellows that was hanging around regular. There was never any meetings. Just: "You going to be in the malt shop tonight?" "Yeah!" There was nothing else you could do.

(Q) *What about the Boys' Club about a mile away from your house? Ever go there when you had nothing else to do?*

(A) You can't go to no Boys' Club. There was probably some kids that went there, to shoot pool or something, but we didn't go. A club, you want to be taken for what you are. You don't want to have to keep your hands clean and do this and don't do that. That's what gets some guys down. They just don't go for stuff like that. These sissy places, a couple guys go there, and they're shooting pool, say. And the cue slips, and one of them says, "Oh, shit!" That's all, boy! Out! They throw you out.

So we kept on hanging out. And the trouble commenced. Picked up for hitching rides. Picked up for curfew. A couple of us was feeling ornery one night, didn't have nothing to do, so we went over and let the air out of some guy's tires. Quite a few times we got picked up for drinking. We got throwed in jail a couple times for fighting at a party. We wasn't fighting, we was arguing. You know, you get a couple, three deals like that and you get so you haven't got a bit of use for cops.

There's another thing. They lock us up for having beer in the car. Why don't they do something about the grownups that sell us the stuff? They're more at fault than we are. If they wasn't to sell it to us we wouldn't be getting drunk, would we?

It's gone on and on like that. I been downtown maybe 125 or 150 times. They just suspended my license, for drunk driving. I run into the side of a house. I got 30 days, license suspended, and now I have to drive without a license.

(Q) *Hank, were there any guys your age, when you started hanging out, who found other things to do? Who didn't hang out?*

(A) Oh, yeah! I'll tell you why that is. Everybody *wants* to hang out when he's a certain age, because he's got to get away from the monotony. Some *don't* hang out because they're scared. They hear you get put in jail if you belong to a gang.

(Q) *You mean there's nobody at all that age who just wouldn't care to belong to a street gang?*

(A) Oh, them! They're scared the group wouldn't accept them. They're the studious type, book worms. What do they do for fun? They go to the show. Make popcorn at home. Cook fudge or something.

(Q) *Well, why would this fellow want to do that while you fellows want to be on the street?*

(A) I don't know what would make you want to hang out. Maybe just one night you went out and had some fun at a party or something and kept on going like that. Maybe you think that's more fun than making fudge. I for damn sure don't care to make fudge!

1. Hank states that "everybody wants to hang out when he's a certain age." From your own experience, would you agree with him? Why or why not? What is that age?

2. Hank does qualify the above statement somewhat when he admits that he did know some boys who didn't "hang out," but that these were either scared or studious. Can you offer any other reasons why individuals might not want to "hang out"?

3. AN IDEALIST LOSES HIS IDEALS *

A young businessman in the used-car business in Chicago describes the process by which he was inducted into crime.

When I graduated from college I had plenty of ideals of honesty, fair play, and cooperation which I had acquired at home, in school, and from literature. My first job after graduation was selling typewriters. During the first day I learned that these machines were not sold at a uniform price but that a person who haggled and waited could get a machine at about half the list price. I felt that this was unfair to the customer who paid the list price. The other salesmen laughed at me and could not understand my silly attitude. They told me to forget the things I had learned in school, and that you couldn't earn a pile of money by being strictly honest. When I replied that money wasn't everything they mocked me: "Oh! No? Well, it helps." I had ideals and I resigned.

My next job was selling sewing machines. I was informed that one machine, which cost the company $18, was to be sold for $40 and another machine, which cost the company $19, was to be sold for $70, and that I was to sell the deluxe model whenever possible in preference to the cheaper model, and was given a list of the reasons why it was a better buy. When I told the sales manager that the business was dishonest and that I was quitting right then, he looked at me as if he thought I was crazy and said angrily: "There's not a cleaner business in the country."

It was quite a time before I could find another job. During this time I occasionally met some of my classmates and they related experiences similar to mine. They said they would starve if they were rigidly honest. All of them had girls and were looking forward to marriage and a com-

* From Edward H. Sutherland, *White Collar Crime.* © 1949 by Holt, Rinehart and Winston. Reprinted by permission of Holt, Rinehart and Winston.

fortable standard of living, and they said they did not see how they could afford to be rigidly honest. My own feelings became less determined than they had been when I quit my first job.

Then I got an opportunity in the used-car business. I learned that this business had more tricks for fleecing customers than either of those I had tried previously. Cars with cracked cylinders, with half the teeth missing from the fly wheel, with everything wrong, were sold as "guaranteed." When the customer returned and demanded his guarantee, he had to sue to get it and very few went to that trouble and expense: the boss said you could depend on human nature. If hot cars could be taken in and sold safely, the boss did not hesitate. When I learned these things I did not quit as I had previously. I sometimes felt disgusted and wanted to quit, but I argued that I did not have much chance to find a legitimate firm. I knew that the game was rotten but it had to be played— the law of the jungle and that sort of thing. I knew that I was dishonest and to that extent felt that I was more honest than my fellows. The thing that struck me as strange was that all these people were proud of their ability to fleece customers. They boasted of their crookedness and were admired by their friends and enemies in proportion to their ability to get away with a crooked deal: it was called shrewdness. Another thing was that these people were unanimous in their denunciation of gangsters, robbers, burglars, and petty thieves. They never regarded themselves as in the same class and were bitterly indignant if accused of dishonesty: it was just good business.

Once in a while, as the years have passed, I have thought of myself as I was in college—idealistic, honest, and thoughtful of others—and have been momentarily ashamed of myself. Before long such memories became less and less frequent and it became difficult to distinguish me from my fellows. If you had accused me of dishonesty I would have denied the charge, but with slightly less vehemence than my fellow businessmen, for after all I had learned a different code of behavior.

What Do You Think?

1. How does the businessman in this episode convince himself to continue in the used car business?

2. One of the statements made by the businessman's boss was that "you could depend on human nature." What do you suppose he meant by that?

3. Do you see any similarity between the individual in this incident and those described in the reading in Chapter 2 entitled "The White Collar Crook"? Explain.

4. BLACK BOY *

Here we have another perspective on the causes of crime. Richard Wright, with his school days completed, describes his attempts to find a job so that he can earn enough money to leave the South of the 1920's. What factors led up to Richard's decision to break the law?

My life now depended upon my finding work, and I was so anxious that I accepted the first offer, a job as a porter in a clothing store selling cheap goods to Negroes on credit. The shop was always crowded with black men and women pawing over cheap suits and dresses. And they paid whatever price the white man asked. The boss, his son, and the clerk treated the Negroes with open contempt, pushing, kicking, or slapping them. No matter how often I witnessed it, I could not get used to it. How can they accept it? I asked myself. I kept on edge, trying to stifle my feelings and never quite succeeding, a prey to guilt and fear because I felt that the boss suspected that I resented what I saw.

One morning, while I was polishing brass out front, the boss and his son drove up in their car. A frightened black woman sat between them. They got out and half dragged and half kicked the woman into the store. White people passed and looked on without expression. A white policeman watched from the corner, twirling his night stick; but he made no move. I watched out of the corner of my eyes, but I never slackened the strokes of my chamois upon the brass. After a moment or two I heard shrill screams coming from the rear room of the store; later the woman stumbled out, bleeding, crying, holding her stomach, her clothing torn. When she reached the sidewalk, the policeman met her, grabbed her, accused her of being drunk, called a patrol wagon and carted her away.

When I went to the rear of the store, the boss and his son were washing their hands at the sink. They looked at me and laughed uneasily. The floor was bloody, strewn with wisps of hair and clothing. My face must have reflected my shock, for the boss slapped me reassuringly on the back.

"Boy, that's what we do to niggers when they don't pay their bills," he said.

His son looked at me and grinned.

---

* Excerpted from Richard Wright, *Black Boy*. New York, N. Y.: Harper & Row, 1945. From pp. 157–160, 170–171, 174–175, 177–181. Copyright 1937, 1942, 1944, 1945 by Richard Wright. Reprinted by permission of Harper & Row, Publishers, Inc.

"Here, have a cigarette," he said.

Not knowing what to do, I took it. He lit his and held the match for me. This was a gesture of kindness, indicating that, even if they had beaten the black woman, they would not beat me if I knew enough to keep my mouth shut.

"Yes, sir," I said.

After they had gone, I sat on the edge of a packing box and stared at the bloody floor until the cigarette went out. . . .

Late one Saturday night I made some deliveries in a white neighborhood. I was pedaling my bicycle back to the store as fast as I could when a police car, swerving toward me, jammed me into the curbing.

"Get down, nigger, and put up your hands!" they ordered.

I did. They climbed out of the car, guns drawn, faces set, and advanced slowly.

"Keep still!" they ordered.

I reached my hands higher. They searched my pockets and packages. They seemed dissatisfied when they could find nothing incriminating. Finally, one of them said:

"Boy, tell your boss not to send you out in white neighborhoods at this time of night."

"Yes, sir," I said.

I rode off, feeling that they might shoot at me, feeling that the pavement might disappear. It was like living in a dream, the reality of which might change at any moment.

Each day in the store I watched the brutality with growing hate, yet trying to keep my feeling from registering in my face. When the boss looked at me I would avoid his eyes. Finally the boss's son cornered me one morning.

"Say, nigger, look here," he began.

"Yes, sir."

"What's on your mind?"

"Nothing, sir," I said, trying to look amazed, trying to fool him.

"Why don't you laugh and talk like the other niggers?" he asked.

"Well, sir, there's nothing much to say or smile about," I said, smiling.

His face was hard, baffled; I knew that I had not convinced him. He whirled from me and went to the front of the store; he came back a moment later, his face red. He tossed a few green bills at me.

"I don't like your looks, nigger. Now get!" he snapped.

I picked up the money and did not count it. I grabbed my hat and left.

For weeks after that I could not believe in my feelings. My personality was numb, reduced to a lumpish, loose, dissolved state. I was a non-man,

something that knew vaguely that it was human but felt that it was not.
. . . What I did feel was a longing to attack. But how? And because I
knew of no way to grapple with this thing, I felt doubly cast out. . . .

But I had to work because I had to eat. My next job was that of a
helper in a drugstore, and the night before I reported for work I fought
with myself, telling myself that I had to master this thing, that my life
depended upon it. Other black people worked, got along somehow, then
I must, *must,* MUST get along until I could get my hands on enough
money to leave. I would make myself fit in. Others had done it. I would
do it. I had to do it.

I went to the job apprehensive, resolving to watch my every move.
I swept the sidewalk, pausing when a white person was twenty feet away.
I mopped the store, cautiously waiting for the white people to move out
of my way in their own good time. I cleaned acres of glass shelving,
changing my tempo now to work faster, holding every nuance of reality
within the focus of my conscious. Noon came and the store was crowded;
people jammed to the counters for food. A white man behind the counter
ran up to me and shouted:

"A jug of Coca-Cola, quick, boy!"

My body jerked taut and I stared at him. He stared at me.

"What's wrong with you?"

"Nothing," I said.

"Well, move! Don't stand there gaping!"

Even if I had tried, I could not have told him what was wrong.
My sustained expectation of violence had exhausted me. My preoccupation with curbing my impulses, my speech, my movements, my manner, my
expressions had increased my anxiety. I became forgetful, concentrating
too much upon trivial tasks. The men began to yell at me and that made
it worse. One day I dropped a jug of orange syrup in the middle of the
floor. The boss was furious. He caught my arm and jerked me into the
back of the drugstore. His face was livid. I expected him to hit me. I
was braced to defend myself.

"I'm going to deduct that from your pay, you black bastard!" he
yelled.

Words had come instead of blows and I relaxed.

"Yes, sir," I said placatingly. "It was my fault."

My tone whipped him to a frenzy.

"You goddamn right it was!" he yelled louder.

"I'm new at this," I mumbled, realizing that I had said the wrong
thing, though I had been striving to say the right.

"We're only trying you out," he warned me.

"Yes, sir. I understand," I said.

He stared at me, speechless with rage. Why could I not learn to keep my mouth shut at the right time? I had said just one short sentence too many. My words were innocent enough, but they indicated, it seemed, a consciousness on my part that infuriated white people.

Saturday night came and the boss gave me my money and snapped: "Don't come back. You won't do."

I knew what was wrong with me, but I could not correct it. The words and actions of white people were baffling signs to me. I was living in a culture and not a civilization and I could learn how that culture worked only by living with it. Misreading the reactions of whites around me made me say and do the wrong things. In my dealing with whites I was conscious of the entirety of my relations with them, and they were conscious only of what was happening at a given moment. I had to keep remembering what others took for granted; I had to think out what others felt. . . .

Out of my salary I had begun to save a few dollars, for my determination to leave had not lessened. But I found the saving exasperatingly slow. I pondered continuously ways of making money, and the only ways that I could think of involved transgressions of the law. No, I must not do that, I told myself. To go to jail in the South would mean the end. And there was the possibility that if I were ever caught I would never reach jail.

This was the first time in my life that I had ever consciously entertained the idea of violating the laws of the land. I had felt that my intelligence and industry could cope with all situations, and, until that time, I had never stolen a penny from anyone. Even hunger had never driven me to appropriate what was not my own. The mere idea of stealing had been repugnant. I had not been honest from deliberate motives, but being dishonest had simply never occurred to me.

Yet, all about me, Negroes were stealing. More than once I had been called a "dumb nigger" by black boys who discovered that I had not availed myself of a chance to snatch some petty piece of white property that had been carelessly left within my reach.

"How in hell you gonna git ahead?" I had been asked when I had said that one ought not steal.

I knew that the boys in the hotel filched whatever they could. I knew that Griggs, my friend who worked in the Capitol Street jewelry store, was stealing regularly and successfully. I knew that a black neighbor of mine was stealing bags of grain from a wholesale house where he worked, though he was a stanch deacon in his church and prayed and sang on Sundays. I knew that the black girls who worked in white homes stole food daily to supplement their scanty wages. And I knew that the very nature of black and white relations bred this constant thievery.

My objections to stealing were not moral. I did not approve of it because I knew that, in the long run, it was futile, that it was not an effective way to alter one's relationship to [one's environment]. Then, how could I change my relationship to my environment? Almost my entire salary went to feed the eternally hungry stomachs at home. If I saved a dollar a week, it would take me two years to amass a hundred dollars, the amount which for some reason I had decided was necessary to stake me in a strange city. And, God knows, anything could happen to me in two years. . . . [Then] a short-cut presented itself. One of the boys at the hotel whispered to me one night that the only local Negro movie house wanted a boy to take tickets at the door.

"You ain't never been in jail, is you?" he asked me.

"Not yet," I answered.

"Then you can get the job," he said. "I'd take it, but I done six months and they know me."

"What's the catch?"

"The girl who sells tickets is using a system," he explained. "If you get the job, you can make some good gravy."

If I stole, I would have a chance to head northward quickly; if I remained barely honest, piddling with pints of bootleg liquor, I merely prolonged my stay, increased my chances of being caught, exposed myself to the possibility of saying the wrong word or doing the wrong thing and paying a penalty that I dared not think of. The temptation to venture into crime was too strong, and I decided to work quickly, taking whatever was in sight, amass a wad of money, and flee. I knew that others had tried it before me and had failed, but I was hoping to be lucky.

My chances for getting the job were good; I had no past record of stealing or violating the laws. When I presented myself to the Jewish proprietor of the movie house I was immediately accepted. The next day I reported for duty and began taking tickets. The boss man warned me:

"Now, look, I'll be honest with you if you'll be honest with me. I don't know who's honest around this joint and who isn't. But if *you* are honest, then the rest are bound to be. All tickets will pass through your hands. There can be no stealing unless you steal."

I gave him a pledge of my honesty, feeling absolutely no qualms about what I intended to do. He was white, and I could never do to him what he and his kind had done to me. Therefore, I reasoned, stealing was not a violation of my ethics, but of his; I felt that things were rigged in his favor and any action I took to circumvent his scheme of life was justified. Yet I had not convinced myself.

During the first afternoon the Negro girl in the ticket office watched me closely and I knew that she was sizing me up, trying to determine when it would be safe to break me into her graft. I waited, leaving it to her to make the first move.

I was supposed to drop each ticket that I took from a customer into a metal receptacle. Occasionally the boss would go to the ticket window and look at the serial number on the roll of unsold tickets and then compare that number with the number on the last ticket I had dropped into the receptacle. The boss continued his watchfulness for a few days, then began to observe me from across the street; finally he absented himself for long intervals.

A tension as high as that I had known when the white men had driven me from the job at the optician's returned to live in me. But I had learned to master a great deal of tension now; I had developed, slowly and painfully, a capacity to contain it within myself without betraying it in any way. Had this not been true, the mere thought of stealing, the risks involved, the inner distress would have so upset me that I would have been in no state of mind to calculate coldly, would have made me so panicky that I would have been afraid to steal at all. But my inner resistance had been blasted. I felt that I had been emotionally cast out of the world, had been made to live outside the normal processes of life, had been conditioned in feeling *against* something daily, had become accustomed to living on the side of those who watched and waited.

While I was eating supper in a near-by cafe one night, a strange Negro man walked in and sat beside me.

"Hello, Richard," he said.

"Hello," I said. "I don't think I know you."

"But I know you," he said, smiling.

Was he one of the boss's spies?

"How do you know me?" I asked.

"I'm Tel's friend," he said, naming the girl who sold the tickets at the movie.

I looked at him searchingly. Was he telling me the truth? Or was he trying to trap me for the boss? I was already thinking and feeling like a criminal, distrusting everybody.

"We start tonight," he said.

"What?" I asked, still not admitting that I knew what he was talking about.

"Don't be scared. The boss trusts you. He's gone to see some friends. Somebody's watching him and if he starts back to the movie, they'll phone us," he said.

I could not eat my food. It lay cold upon the plate and sweat ran down from my armpits.

"It'll work this way," he explained in a low, smooth tone. "A guy'll come to you and ask for a match. You give him five tickets that you'll hold out of the box, see? We'll give you the signal when to start holding out. The guy'll give the tickets to Tel; she'll resell them all at once, when a crowd is buying at the rush hour. You get it?"

I did not answer. I knew that if I were caught I would go to the chain gang. But was not my life already a kind of chain gang? What, really, did I have to lose?

"Are you with us?" he asked.

I still did not answer. He rose and clapped me on the shoulder and left. I trembled as I went back to the theater. Anything might happen, but I was used to that. . . . Had I not felt it all a million times before? I took the tickets with sweaty fingers. I waited. I was gambling: freedom or the chain gang. There were times when I felt that I could not breathe. I looked up and down the street; the boss was not in sight. Was this a trap? If it were, I would disgrace my family. Would not all of them say that my attitude had been leading to this all along? Would they not rake up the past and find clues that had led to my fate?

The man I had met in the cafe came through the door and put a ticket in my hand.

"There's a crowd at the box office," he whispered. "Save ten, not five. Start with this one."

Well, here goes, I thought. He gave me the ticket and sat looking at the moving shadows upon the screen. I held on to the ticket and my body grew tense, hot as fire; but I was used to that too. Time crawled through the cells of my brain. My muscles ached. I discovered that crime means suffering. The crowd came in and gave me more tickets. I kept ten of them tucked into my moist palm. No sooner had the crowd thinned than a black boy with a cigarette jutting from his mouth came up to me.

"Gotta match?"

With a slow movement I gave him the tickets. He went out and I kept the door cracked and watched. He went to the ticket office and laid down a coin and I saw him slip the tickets to the girl. Yes, the boy was honest. The girl shot me a quick smile and I went back inside. A few moments later the same tickets were handed to me by other customers.

We worked it for a week and after the money was split four ways, I had fifty dollars. Freedom was almost within my grasp. Ought I risk any more? I dropped the hint to Tel's friend that maybe I would quit; it was a casual hint to test him out. He grew violently angry and I quickly consented to stay, fearing that someone might turn me in for revenge, or to get me out of the way so that another and more pliable boy could have my place. I was dealing with cagey people and I would be cagey.

I went through another week. Late one night I resolved to make that week the last. The gun in the neighbor's house came to my mind, and the cans of fruit preserves in the storehouse of the college. If I stole them and sold them, I would have enough to tide me over in Memphis until I could get a job, work, save, and go north. I crept from bed and found the neighbor's house empty. I looked about; all was quiet. My heart beat so fast that it ached. I forced a window with a screwdriver and entered and took the gun; I slipped it in my shirt and returned home. When I took it out to look at it, it was wet with sweat. I pawned it under an assumed name.

The following night I rounded up two boys whom I knew to be ready for adventure. We broke into the college storehouse and lugged out cans of fruit preserves and sold them to restaurants.

Meanwhile I bought clothes, shoes, a cardboard suitcase, all of which I hid at home. Saturday night came and I sent word to the boss that I was sick. Uncle Tom was upstairs. Granny and Aunt Addie were at church. My brother was sleeping. My mother sat in her rocking chair, humming to herself. I packed my suitcase and went to her.

"Mama, I'm going away," I whispered.

"Oh, no," she protested.

"I've got to, mama. I can't live this way."

"You're not running away from something you've done?"

"I'll send for you, mama. I'll be all right."

"Take care of yourself. And send for me quickly. I'm not happy here," she said.

"I'm sorry for all these long years, mama. But I could not have helped it."

I kissed her and she cried.

"Be quiet, mama. I'm all right."

I went out the back way and walked a quarter of a mile to the railroad tracks. It began to rain as I tramped down the crossties toward town. I reached the station soaked to the skin. I bought my ticket, then went hurriedly to the corner of the block in which the movie house stood. Yes, the boss was there, taking the tickets himself. I returned to the station and waited for my train, my eyes watching the crowd.

An hour later I was sitting in a Jim Crow coach, speeding northward, making the first lap of my journey to a land where I could live with a little less fear. Slowly the burden I had carried for many months lifted somewhat. My cheeks itched and when I scratched them I found tears. In that moment I understood the pain that accompanied crime and I hoped that I would never have to feel it again. I never did feel it again, for I never stole again; and what kept me from it was the knowledge that, for me, crime carried its own punishment.

What Do You Think?

1. What factors contributed to Richard's feeling that he was a "non-man"? Might some people feel like this today? Explain.

2. What led Richard to join in the plan to steal from the movie theater? Were there other alternatives open to him? Explain.

3. Richard states that he never stole again because of the knowledge that, for him, crime carried its own punishment. What do you think he meant by that statement? Would you agree with him? Why or why not?

5. "I LIKE THE MONEY, BUT I LIKE TO HEAR THEM BEG MORE" *

An investigator from McCall's magazine managed to interview a group of young narcotics addicts in New York City. Their habits cost an average of $30.00 a day, which they obtained through illegal activities, though the reporter did not inquire about specific crimes. In several of these cases, too, cruelty, rather than the need for dope alone, appeared to be a major motivation. What does this brief excerpt imply to be a cause of crime?

"I like the money, but I like to hear them beg more," said one addict about his victims. A Negro remarked: "When I feel the dope in me, I go. I'm free, and everybody look out." Another spoke of his penchant for attacking small victims: "Oh, do I like to hit the small ones! They scream the loudest. Small and scared, but with big mouths, like my old lady." Said a fourth: "I feel like a vampire sometimes, swooping down and hitting people at night. I take their blood because I need it. But I haven't figured out what I need it for. And when I've got it, I don't want it, but I have to have it, or I'll want it some more."

What Do You Think?

Do you think that some people really enjoy being cruel for cruelty's sake alone? What factors might produce this type of cruelty in an individual?

6. TOO MUCH COMPASSION FOR 'PUNKS' *

Pity for criminals sometimes exceeds our concern for the victims of crime, argues Bishop Fulton J. Sheen. Could this be a cause of crime?

Crime is increasing, says the Most Reverend Fulton J. Sheen, because of a widespread and "false compassion" for criminals.

Bishop Sheen, a leading philosopher of the Roman Catholic Church and the Bishop of Rochester, defines false compassion in these words:

---

* Excerpted from Samuel Grafton, "The Crime That Threatens Every Woman," *McCall's Magazine*, February 1965. Copyright 1965 *McCall's Magazine*. Reprinted by permission McCall Corporation, Inc.
* Excerpted from Bishop Fulton J. Sheen, "Too Much Compassion for Punks," *U. S. News & World Report*, January 23, 1967. Copyright 1967 *U. S. News & World Report*.

"A pity that is shown, not to the mugged, but to the mugger; not to the family of the murdered, but to the murderer; not to the woman who was raped, but to the rapist."

This attitude, Bishop Sheen said in a telecast carried by a number of U.S. stations, is responsible to a large degree for the rising crime rate in the U.S. and the fact that twelve out of every 100 policemen were assaulted last year.

"Social slobberers" were deplored by the Bishop as those "who insist on compassion being shown to the junkies, to the dope fiends, the throat slashers, the beatniks, the prostitutes, the homosexuals, and the punks. Today the decent man is practically off the reservation."

Bishop Sheen noted that crime is increasing because "clemency of a false kind is shown to criminals."

This is the picture he described:

"There is a robbery in the United States every 30 seconds. There is an auto stolen every minute. A rape is committed every three minutes. A murder is perpetrated in the United States every 60 minutes."

The Bishop declared that 43 per cent of those arrested for robbery and larceny have already received earlier clemency.

"In New York City alone," he said, "there are 60,000 narcotic addicts. Of all those that are arrested for dope-pushing, selling, taking narcotics, 37 per cent are released."

Bishop Sheen concluded that part of the blame for this crime picture "has to be laid at the door of all of those who have committed and shown false compassion."

What Do You Think?

1.   What appears to be the Bishop's diagnosis as to the cause of crime? Would you agree with him or not? Why?

2.   Compare the views of Bishop Sheen with those of Miller in the next article. With whose would you agree? Why?

7.   THE BORED AND THE VIOLENT *

In this article, Arthur Miller, one of America's foremost playwrights, argues that there is a "spirit gone." What do you think he means? Can this spirit be recaptured?

---

* Excerpted from Arthur Miller, "The Bored and the Violent," *Harper's Magazine,* November 1962. Reprinted by permission of Ashley Famous Agency, Inc. Copyright © 1962 *Harper's Magazine.*

No one knows what "causes" delinquency. Having spent some months in the streets with boys of an American gang, I came away with certain impressions, all of which stemmed from a single, overwhelming conviction —that the problem underneath is boredom. And it is not strange, after all, that this should be so. It is the theme of so many of our novels, our plays, and especially our movies in the past twenty years, and is the hallmark of society as a whole. The outcry of Britain's so-called Angry Young Men was against precisely this seemingly universal sense of life's pointlessness, the absence of any apparent aim to it all. So many American books and articles attest to the same awareness here. The stereotype of the man coming home from work and staring dumbly at a television set is an expression of it, and the "New Wave" of movies in France and Italy propound the same fundamental theme. People no longer seem to know why they are alive; existence is simply a string of near-experience . . . and the good life is basically an amused one.

Among the delinquents the same kind of mindlessness prevails, but without the style—or stylishness—which art in our time has attempted to give it. The boredom of the delinquent is remarkable mainly because it is so little compensated for, as it may be among the middle classes and the rich who can fly down to the Caribbean or to Europe, or refurnish the house, or have an affair, or at least go shopping. The delinquent is stuck with his boredom, stuck inside it, stuck to it, until for two or three minutes he "lives"; he goes on a raid around the corner and feels the thrill of risking his skin or his life as he smashes a bottle filled with gasoline on some other kid's head. In a sense, it is his trip to Miami. It makes his day. It is his shopping tour. It gives him something to talk about for a week. It is *life*. Standing around with nothing coming up is as close to dying as you can get. Unless one grasps the power of boredom, the threat of it to one's existence, it is impossible to "place" the delinquent as a member of the human race.

With boredom in the forefront, one may find some perspective in the melange of views which are repeated endlessly about the delinquent. He is a rebel without a cause, or a victim of poverty, or a victim of undue privilege, or an unloved child, or an overloved child, or a child looking for a father, or a child trying to avenge himself on an uncaring society, or whatnot. But face to face with one of them, one finds these criteria useless, if only because no two delinquents are any more alike than other people are. They do share one mood, however. They are drowning in boredom. School bores them, preaching bores them, even television bores them. The word rebel is inexact for them because it must inevitably imply a purpose, an end.

Other people, of course, have known boredom. To get out of it, they go to the movies, or to a bar, or read a book, or go to sleep, or turn on TV or a girl, or make a resolution, or quit a job. Younger persons who are not delinquents may go to their room and weep, or write a poem, or call up a friend until they get tired talking. But note that each of these escapes can only work if the victim is sure somewhere in his mind, or reasonably hopeful, that by so doing he will overthrow his boredom and with luck may come out on the other side where something hopeful or interesting waits. But the delinquent has no such sense of an imminent improvement. . . . [Many delinquents] have never known a single good day. How can they be expected to project one and restrain themselves in order to experience such joy once more?

The word rebel is wrong, too, in that it implies some sort of social criticism in the delinquent. But . . . the delinquent has only respect, even reverence, for certain allegedly bourgeois values. He implicitly believes that there are good girls and bad girls, for instance. Sex and marriage are two entirely separate things. He is, in my experience anyway, deeply patriotic. Which is simply to say that he respects those values he never experienced, like money and good girls and the Army and Navy. What he has experienced has left him with absolute contempt, or more accurately, an active indifference. Once he does experience decency—as he does sometimes in a wife—he reacts decently to it. For to this date the only known cure for delinquency is marriage.

The delinquent, far from being the rebel, is the conformist par excellence. He is actually incapable of doing anything alone, and a story may indicate how incapable he is. I went along with [a delinquent] gang to a YMCA camp outside New York City for an overnight outing. In the afternoon we started a baseball game, and everything proceeded normally until somebody hit a ball to the outfield. I turned to watch the play and saw ten or twelve kids running for the catch. It turned out that not one of them was willing to play the outfield by himself, insisting that the entire group hang around out there together. The reason was that a boy alone might drop a catch and would not be able to bear the humiliation. So they ran around out there in a drove all afternoon, creating a stampede every time a ball was hit.

They are frightened kids, and that is why they are so dangerous. But again, it will not do to say—it is simply not true—that they are therefore unrelated to the rest of the population's frame of mind. Like most of us, the delinquent is simply doing as he was taught. This is often said but rarely understood. Only recently a boy was about to be executed for murder in New York State. Only after he had been in jail for more than a year after sentencing did a campaign develop to persuade the Governor to commute his sentence to life imprisonment, for only then was it discovered that he had been deserted by his father in Puerto Rico, left behind when his mother went to New York, wandered about homeless throughout his childhood, and so on. The sentencing judge only learned his background a week or two before he was to be officially murdered. And then what shock, what pity! I have to ask why the simple facts of his deprivation were not brought out in court, if not before. I am afraid I know the answer. Like most people, it was probably beyond the judge's imagination that small children sometimes can be treated much worse than kittens or puppies in our cities.

Gangs in Suburbia

It is only in theory that the solution seems purely physical—better housing, enlightened institutions for deserted kids, psychotherapy, and the rest. The visible surfaces of the problem are easy to survey—although we have hardly begun even to do that.

More difficult is the subterranean moral question which every kind of delinquency poses. Not long ago a gang was arrested in a middle-class section of Brooklyn, whose task was to rob homes and sell the stuff to professional fences. Many of these boys were top students, and all of them were from good, middle-class backgrounds. Their parents were floored by the news of their secret depredations, and their common cry was that they had always given their sons plenty of money, that the boys were secure at home, that there was no conceivable reason for this kind of aberration. The boys were remorseful and evidently as bewildered as their parents.

Greenwich, Connecticut, is said to be the wealthiest community in the United States. A friend of mine who lives there let his sons throw a party for their friends. In the middle of the festivities a gang of boys arrived—their own acquaintances who attend the same high school. They tore the house apart, destroyed the furniture, pulled parts off the automobile and left them on the lawn, and split the skulls of two of the guests with beer cans.

Now if it is true that the slum delinquent does as he is taught, it must be true that the Greenwich delinquent does the same. But . . . it is doubtful that the parents of this marauding gang rip up the furniture in the homes to which they have been invited. So that once again it is necessary to withhold one's cherished theories. Rich delinquency is delinquency but it is not the same as slum delinquency. But there is one clear common denominator, I think. They do not know how to live when alone. Most boys in Greenwich do not roam in gangs but a significant fraction in both places find that counterfeit sense of existence which the gang life provides.

Again, I think it necessary to raise and reject the idea of rebellion, if one means by that word a thrust of any sort. For perspective's sake it may be wise to remember another kind of youthful reaction to a failed society in a different era. In the 'thirties, for instance, we were also contemptuous of the given order. We had been brought up to believe that if you worked hard, saved your money, studied, kept your nose clean, you would end up made. We found ourselves in the Depression, when you could not get a job, when all the studying you might do would get you a chance, at best, to sell ties in Macy's. Our delinquency consisted in joining demonstrations of the unemployed, pouring onto campuses to scream against some injustice by college administrations, and adopting to one degree or another a Socialist ideology. This, in fact, was a more dangerous kind of delinquency than the gangs imply, for it was directed against the social structure of capitalism itself. But, curiously, it was at the same time immeasurably more constructive, for the radical youth of the 'thirties, contemptuous as he was of the social values he had rejected, was still bent upon instituting human values in their place. He was therefore a conserver, he believed in *some* society.

To think of contemporary delinquency in the vein of the 'thirties, as a rebellion toward something, is to add a value to it which it does not have. To give it even the dignity of cynicism run rampant is also over elaborate. For the essence is not the individual at all; it is the gang, the herd, and we should be able to understand its attractions ourselves. It is not the thrust toward individual expression but a flight from self in any defined form. Therefore, to see it simply as a protest against conformism is to stand it on its head; it is profoundly conformist.

The Greenwich gang, therefore, is also doing as it was taught, just as the slum gang does, but more subtly. The Greenwich gang is conforming to the hidden inhumanity of conformism, to the herd quality in conformism; it is acting out the terror-fury that lies hidden under father's acceptable conformism. It is simply conformity sincere, conformity revealing its true content, which is hatred of others, a stunted wish for omnipotence, and the conformist's secret belief that nothing outside his skin is real or true. For which reason he must redouble his obeisance to institutions lest, if the act of obeisance be withheld, the whole external world will vanish, leaving him alone. And to be left alone when you do not sense any existence in yourself is the ultimate terror. This loneliness is a withdrawal not from the world but from oneself. It is boredom, the subsidence of inner impulse, and it threatens true death unless it is overthrown.

All of which is said in order to indicate that delinquency is not the kind of "social problem" it is generally thought to be. That is, it transcends even as it includes the need for better housing, medical care, and the rest. It is our most notable and violent manifestation of social nihilism. In saying this, however, it is necessary to short-circuit any notion that it is an attempt by the youth to live "sincerely." The air of "sincerity"

which so many writers have given the delinquent is not to be
as his "purpose." This is romanticism and solves nothing except
mentalize brutality. The gang kid can be sincere; he can exten[?]
for a buddy and risk himself for others; but he is just as liable, if not
more so than others, to desert his buddies in need and to treat his friends
disloyally. Gang boys rarely go to visit a buddy in jail excepting in the
movies. They forget about him. The cult of sincerity, of true human
relations uncontaminated by money and the social rat race, is not the
hallmark of the gang. The only moment of truth comes when the war
starts. Then the brave show themselves, but few of these boys know
how to fight alone, and hardly any without a knife or a gun. They are
not to be equated with matadors or boxers, or Hemingway heroes. They
are dangerous pack hounds who will not even expose themselves singly in
the outfield.

Flight from Nothingness

If, then, one begins to put together all the elements, this "social
problem" . . . is not a problem of big cities alone but of rural areas too;
not of capitalism alone but of socialism as well; not restricted to the
physically deprived but shared by the affluent; not a racial problem alone
or a problem of recent immigrants, or a purely American problem. I
believe it is in its present form the product of technology destroying the
very concept of man as a value in himself.

I hesitate to say what I think the cure might be, if only because
I cannot prove it. But I have heard most of the solutions men have offered,
and they are spiritless, they do not assume that the wrong is deep and
terrible and general among us all. There is, in a word, a spirit gone.
Perhaps two world wars, brutality immeasurable, have blown it off the
earth; perhaps the very processes of technology have sucked it out of
man's soul; but it is gone. Many men rarely relate to one another excepting
as customer to seller, worker to boss, the affluent to the deprived and
vice versa—in short, as factors to be somehow manipulated and not as
intrinsically valuable persons.

Power was always in the world, to be sure, and its evils, but with
us now it is strangely . . . masked and distorted. Time was, for example,
when the wealthy and the politically powerful flaunted themselves, used
power openly as power, and were often cruel. But this openness had the
advantage for men of clarity; it created a certain reality in the world,
an environment that was defined, with hard but touchable barriers. Today
power would have us believe—everywhere—that it is purely beneficent.
The bank is not a place which makes more money with your deposits
than it returns to you in the form of interest; it is not a sheer economic

necessity, it is not a business at all. It is "Your Friendly Bank," a kind of welfare institution whose one prayer, day and night, is to serve your whims or needs. A school is no longer a place of mental discipline but a kind of day-care center, a social gathering where you go through a ritual of games and entertainments which insinuate knowledge and the crafts of the outside world. Business is not the practice of buying low and selling high, it is a species of public service. The good life itself is not the life of struggle for meaning, not the quest for union with the past, with God, with man that it traditionally was. The good life is the life of ceaseless entertainment and effortless joys. . . . Freedom is, after all, comfort; sexuality is a photograph. The enemy of it all is the real. The enemy is conflict. The enemy, in a word, is life.

My own view is that delinquency is related to this dreamworld from two opposing sides. There are the deprived who cannot take part in the dream; poverty bars them. There are the oversated who are caught in its indefiniteness, its unreality, its boring hum, and strike for the real now and then—they rob, they hurt, they kill. In flight from the nothingness of this comfort they have inherited, they butt against its rubber walls in order to feel a real pain, a genuine consequence. For the world in which comfort rules is a delusion, whether one is within it or deprived of it. . . .

I do not know how we ought to reach for the spirit again but it seems to me we must flounder without it. It is the spirit which does not accept injustice complacently and yet does not betray the poor with sentimentality. It is the spirit which seeks not to flee the tragedy which life must always be, but seeks to enter into it, thereby to be strengthened by the fullest awareness of its pain. It is the spirit which does not mask but unmasks the true function of a thing, be it business, unionism, architecture, or love.

[There have been some good solutions]: Reform of idiotic narcotics laws, a real attempt to put trained people at the service of bewildered, desperate families, job-training programs, medical care, reading clinics— all of [these are] necessary and none . . . would so much as strain our economy. But none will matter, none . . . will reach further than the spirit in which [they are] done. Not the spirit of fear with which so many face delinquency, nor the spirit of sentimentality which sees in it some virtue of rebellion against a false and lying society. The spirit has to be that of those people who know that delinquents are a living expression of our universal ignorance of what life ought to be, even of what it is, and of what it truly means to live. Bad pupils they surely are. But who from his own life, from his personal thought has come up with the good teaching, the way of life that is joy? It is [difficult] to reach these boys; what the country has to decide is what it is going to say if these kids should decide to listen.

1. Could Arthur Miller use Hank (as described in the first reading in this chapter) as an example of what he feels to be the basic problem underlying juvenile delinquency? Explain.
2. Would you agree with Miller's statement that the delinquent is the "conformist par excellence"? Why or why not? What evidence could you present to either support or refute the statement?
3. Do you think it is true that many individuals today do not know how to live when alone? What factors in our society might contribute to this?
4. How do you think we might begin to bring about the solution to the problem (that is, of juvenile delinquency) which Miller proposes?

8. WHO CARES? *

Leonard Gross, a senior editor for LOOK magazine, argues that we (meaning all of us) have got to care. What does he mean? What does "caring" have to do with the causes of crime?

This country . . . has begun to wonder if its people will save one another.

The growth of this suspicion can be clearly traced. It was born in New York City at 3:25 A.M. last March 13, when a man attacked 28-year-old Catherine Genovese as she was returning to her home from work. He stabbed her. She screamed for help, and he fled. Twice in the next half hour, he returned to stab her. Repeatedly, she called to her neighbors for help. At least 38 of them heard her, but none of them helped her, and she died.

The story stunned the nation. In succeeding weeks, newspapers the country over produced local versions of what had all the appearances of an epidemic of apathy. Examples:

In Chicago, 60 persons ignored a uniformed policeman's cries for assistance as he battled two youths. In Santa Clara, California, several motorists saw a taxicab driver being robbed, but none even summoned police. In San Pedro, California, other motorists drove by two police-

* Leonard Gross, "Who Cares?" *Look,* September 8, 1964. Copyright 1964 Cowles Communications, Inc.

men struggling to prevent a man from jumping off a 185-foot-high bridge. "We were hanging on for dear life and trying to get someone to stop. But they all drove on like they didn't want to be bothered or get involved," one of the patrolmen reported later. Back in New York City, a Broadway crowd stood by while eight men stomped two; a Bronx crowd would not rescue a naked girl from a rapist's attack, and bystanders fled from a 19-year-old college student who had just been stabbed by one member of a gang of toughs. His statement to the New York *Times* is unforgettable:

"I put my hand down and saw blood. I went over to a car that had stopped to watch. 'Please help me to a hospital,' I said. They rolled up their windows and drove away. I went to another car and asked for help, but they did the same thing, drove away. Then I went to a truck and asked the driver for help. He pulled around me and drove away and left me there. Nobody on the street helped me."

Who cares? Seldom in our history has a question so un-American seemed so necessary. It strikes at the jugular of our national life—our historic readiness to sacrifice personal safety for the public good.

Who cares? Millions of Americans do, a national survey by *Look* indicates—the swollen ranks of volunteer charity workers, the battlers for civil rights, the numerous civilian heroes and the unnumbered Americans who, seeing danger, summon police. Rochester, Detroit, Atlanta, St. Louis, San Francisco—these and many other cities report excellent citizen cooperation. Even in New York, where a single telephone call would have saved Catherine Genovese, there were 436,149 cases last year in which one or more persons summoned help.

Who cares? An unknown number of Americans do not—not, at least, enough to act. To the widely publicized incidents above can be added innumerable incidents uncovered by *Look*. Some can be excused because those who failed to act may not have understood what was happening, or did not know what to do. But most such incidents cannot be excused at all. "The fact that they do happen is a danger signal," says Dr. Arnold Abrams, a Chicago Medical School clinical psychologist. That there is an epidemic of noninvolvement is unlikely; that there is a problem is irrefutable. It must be explained.

Many explanations are being offered. All of them make some sense. None is very pleasant. One is that Americans are becoming too dollar-minded to risk the costs of involvement. Getting involved means being a witness. You lose time, pay, even popularity. A man in a building close to the one in which the young girl from the Bronx was raped railed at reporters for calling attention to the story. It was bad for business, he said. Now women wouldn't come to his office anymore. In New Orleans, Mabel Simmons, book-page editor of the *Times-Picayune,* saw a woman lying, apparently unconscious, on a sidewalk in the city's business district. No one seemed too concerned. Mrs. Simmons went into a nearby store, where she received permission to call the police. When they asked for the address, she, in turn, asked the store owner. He refused to give it to her. He didn't want the store connected with a police incident. In disgust, she set down the phone and checked the address herself.

Fear of involvement is widespread and pronounced. Sometimes, it is the fear of hurting someone. More often, it is the fear of getting hurt. One veteran social worker reports, "If a boy is stabbed in the hallway of a project, he can die, and no one will help him. They're all afraid of retaliation." Many Americans are loath to testify at trials, and serve on juries with reluctance. Judge Nathan M. Cohen of Chicago's Criminal Court excused more than 200 persons before he could complete a jury to hear a recent case involving organized crime. Male prospects asking to be released spoke in low voices, fidgeted with their clothing and refused to look the judge in the eye. The case was finally heard by an all-woman jury.

In a New Orleans suburb two years ago, a young girl was leaning over her hi-fi set when a bullet shot past her head. Outside, residents found two drunken constables shooting off their guns. But no one—not even the girl's parents—reported the incident to authorities. "We didn't know when we might need them," someone said lamely.

Enforcement authorities blame cumbersome legal processes and a tendency to "understand" rather than punish criminals as causes of citizen reluctance. Despairing of getting satisfaction, people do not press charges. But at least one veteran police chief, Edward J. Allen of Santa Ana, California, cites the police themselves as one source of the problem. "They don't integrate. They develop a feeling that they have been set aside by society," he contends. Whatever the causes, there is a decisive feeling of estrangement between the public and law-enforcement agencies that accounts, in part, for the phenomenon of noninvolvement.

Another suggestion offered by authorities is that because we are now provided for in so many ways, the principle of individual responsibility is vanishing from American life.

Aaron M. Kohn, managing director of the New Orleans Metropolitan Crime Commission, Inc., speaks with dismay about the "metropolitan complex," which enables the citizen to rationalize away his obligations to society. Dr. Joel Elkes, psychiatrist-in-chief of The Johns Hopkins Hospital in Baltimore, decries the synthetic quality of contemporary experience, "when staring at the TV replaces good talk with a neighbor; or the phonograph, community singing in the church hall; or the latest what-to-do-next book on child-rearing, a real involvement with one's children." So much do we simulate, says Dr. Elkes, that when a real, live situation impels action, we are out of the acting habit. In Las Vegas, Nevada, some time ago, a Federal narcotics undercover agent was shot while sitting in his car in a residential neighborhood. Many people ran to their doors and peered into the darkness, but none of them ventured outside to investigate. When police asked later why they hadn't, several explained they had been watching *The Untouchables* on television and wanted to see the end of the program.

A frequently mentioned source of noninvolvement is what the technicians call "a breakdown in primary groups"—groups united by culture, language, religion, or common purpose. One American in four moves every year, the small-town resident to the city in search of opportunity, the city dweller to the suburbs in search for peace. In his new environment, he feels no identity, sinks no roots, has no stake. Strangeness frightens him; feeling threatened, he seeks to eliminate risks. He stays in line; he conforms. His world is now so complex that "the only way to survive is to cut a lot of it out," says Dr. Alfred J. Kahn, professor of social-welfare planning at Columbia University. Adds Alvin L. Schorr, a research chief of the Social Security Administration, "The man doesn't want to do too much. He adjusts by shutting things out. It may not work for society. But it works for him."

The problem appears to be greatest in cities where a sense of community is lowest. California's Bay Area offers a striking example. San Francisco is noted for the community pride of its residents. Police Chief Thomas J. Cahill speaks glowingly about the cooperation he receives from the public. If an assault of the Catherine Genovese type occurred in San Francisco? "We'd get fifty calls in five minutes." Oakland, across the Bay, is an unobtrusive city with many migrants and little civic verve. Its police chief, E. M. Toothman, lists 10 recent cases of public refusal to become involved—including one in which at least six persons failed to help a 63-year-old man who was being fatally stomped—and offers some dejected views about the moral breakdown of society.

When an individual leaves the neighborhood that knows him, he loses his first line of defense. The New York college student who was stabbed is probably alive today because he managed to make his way to his own block, where neighbors summoned aid.

The relationship of an aroused, unified neighborhood to individual safety shows clearly in the recent history of Hyde Park on Chicago's South Side. Once a secure, middle-class area dominated by the beautiful University of Chicago campus, Hyde Park by 1953 had become a lair of muggers. So unsafe were the streets that the existence of the university itself was threatened. Then one crime—the abduction and disrobing of a woman—aroused the neighborhood. Hyde Park's residents, including some of the best minds in the country, mapped a cleanup. The community was organized. Slums were razed, and new row houses built. A gospel of cooperation was preached. Today Hyde Park is the envy of neighborhoods around it. Such is the sense of community that a cry for help brings instant action. Responding to a scream one evening this spring, sociologist Philip Hauser rushed from his house to find a number of his neighbors, all brandishing baseball bats, fire pokers, and other makeshift weapons, chasing a would-be purse snatcher down the street. "I doubt that he tried Hyde Park again," says Hauser. Such community response has helped cut the crime rate nearly 50 per cent since 1953.

"Success can be found only where there exists citizen zeal," states *Mental Health in the Metropolis,* the work of several prominent scholars. "What is needed is community feeling—when inhabitants have a *central* feeling of belonging."

But the problem is that tendencies in our society are leading us away from the kind of life in which community feelings can flourish. As we move further from old ways, we must rely more and more on the individual's will to act.

"The self-image is what propels one—if one has it," says psychiatrist Elkes of Johns Hopkins. "One gets it from the expected sources —father and mother, primarily, teacher and preacher as well. If that self-image is strong enough, it makes you confront events you would rather avoid. You call the police. You stop and give aid. At times, you even take risks."

To a man, the authorities counseling *Look* agree that the question of willingness to take risks, of individual responsibility, goes back to some pretty old-fashioned fundamentals in human relationships.

If you don't pick up a telephone, it's pretty certain that your son won't either. "He doesn't receive the cues, if you don't give them to him," says Dr. Elkes. If you counsel him to conform, get by, keep his nose clean, you'll find he sticks pretty closely to such advice. In Chicago last summer, 5'4" Royace Prather smashed a chair over the head of an armed 6-foot robber who was holding up a restaurant cashier. Analyzing his motives recently, he recalled his father, a farmer "who tried to treat people nicely. He got mad at me one time, I remember, when I forgot to say thanks on the telephone to someone when I was in high school. He always returned borrowed things in better shape than he got them. He always believed in helping people."

In the end, the man who responds is the man who feels something for others. If a child is loved, he can take the risk of loving—or helping —others in turn. "You've got to be able to believe that you can get involved in the lives of others without getting hurt," says a Washington, D. C., psychologist.

The man on the sidelines may well be one who was never given a sense of his own worth. Such a man cannot appreciate the worth of others. When others are in trouble, he will not respond.

Clearly, the emerging problem of noninvolvement in the United States is not simply a matter of human indifference. "Apathy is not the right word," says Dan Carpenter, executive director of the Hudson Guild Settlement House in New York City. "Apparent indifference can be a form of protection, a defense mechanism." Because a man on shore does not rush into the water to save another man from drowning does not necessarily mean that he is apathetic. It may simply mean that he can't swim.

The events of recent months are not an indictment. But they *are* a warning. They have exposed a dangerous incapacity in our society of which we have largely been unaware. We are living in a new world, and we are being tested everywhere—in Vietnam, New York, Mississippi— in ways we have never been before. The rediscovery that we need one another, that we are involved in all mankind, that we have got to care, could atone in part for the murder of Catherine Genovese.

What Do You Think?

1. Does Mr. Gross make his case that many Americans do not "care"? What does he mean by this statement? Can you refute his argument?
2. Compare Gross's article with the one by Arthur Miller. What similarities and differences can you find? Explain.
3. Imagine that you are being interviewed by a correspondent from a foreign newspaper. How would you explain the fact that thirty-eight eyewitnesses to the Genovese attack did not call the police?
4. Gross states that we (Americans) are being tested everywhere. What does he mean? Would you agree? Why or why not?

9.   THE SEARCH FOR EXPLANATIONS: SOME THEORIES WHICH TRY TO EXPLAIN WHAT CAUSES CRIME

There have been many explanations offered as to the causes of crime. Though none of these theories are wholly satisfactory, they do provide some insights into the factors which contribute to crime and criminal behavior. What follows are a number of theories for you to consider, presented in somewhat simplified form.

A. The Idea of "Constitutional Inferiority"

Criminals are a born physical type who have inherited a tendency toward criminal behavior, and who possess certain unusual physical features by which they can be identified. Such features include a flat head, a large jaw with an unusually long or receding chin, a distorted nose, big, protruding ears, large lips, long arms, and many others. No criminal would have all of these identifying characteristics, but he would possess considerably more than the average individual. These physical character- istics, moreover, indicate mental inferiority which is the result of defec- tive heredity rather than social circumstances. It is difficult for the criminal type, therefore, not to engage in criminal behavior. In essence, the theory holds that "criminals are born, not made."

B. The Relationship Between I.Q. and Crime

Persons with low I.Q.'s are more likely than those with average and above average I.Q.'s to turn to crime. This is supported by the fact that a number of early studies of I.Q.'s revealed that a large proportion of the inmates of penitentiaries were either defective or "dull normal." Crime, therefore, is essentially a by-product of intellectual inadequacy.

C. Personality Disorganization and Crime

Delinquency and crime are caused by emotional problems which disorga- nize the individual's personality. These problems, such as insecurity, in- adequacy, or a sense of rejection, are caused by inner conflicts created in early life through an unsatisfactory family alliance. Since the most important associations are those which occur during early childhood, the relationships during the formative years with one's parents and siblings have an almost indelible effect on an individual's personality. If they are unsatisfying, they can lead to deviant behavior. Since the inner conflicts rest below the level of consciousness, the individual is usually incapable of understanding why he acts as he does, or how to change his actions. Crime, therefore, represents a pattern of conduct which is essentially a symptom of underlying emotional problems.

D. The Poverty Theory

Behavior is not determined by the individual himself, but rather by forces over which he has little control. Though he may have some choice in directing the course of his life, the choices open to him are consider- ably limited by his external environment. People are not good or bad as such. They respond to the impersonal effects of economic and social forces outside themselves. Poverty, in particular, is likely to lead to a life of crime.

Inadequate clothing and shelter, insufficient food and resulting mal- nutrition, along with other problems coupled with despair of escaping these conditions, frequently result in demoralization, deviancy, and crimi- nality.

E. The Differential Association Theory

Criminal behavior is learned. It is learned through associating and communicating on an intimate basis with criminals. Through such contacts, the individual learns a different code of behavior and a different set of techniques, attitudes, motives, and rationalizations. These associations vary in terms of how early they occur, their frequency, duration, and intensity. An individual becomes a criminal once he accepts and internalizes a set of definitions of the legal code more favorable to violation than to obedience.

F. Sub-cultural Explanations

"INVERSION" OF MIDDLE CLASS NORMS

The majority of lower class boys face two choices; they can, primarily through higher education, try to move into the middle class, or they can accept their lower class status, insulate themselves as much as possible from middle class ways of life, and perpetuate their accustomed way of life. This latter group eventually become skilled, semi-skilled, or unskilled workers in adult life.

Some lower class boys, however, can make neither of these adjustments. Instead they lash out at what they cannot attain, and come to reject middle class norms and values. They then become delinquents, often stealing for stealing's sake. They delight in malicious behavior (such as slashing tires). They set their standards exactly opposite from what is accepted in the middle class culture, rejecting conventional authority figures, and living for the pleasure of the moment.

LOWER CLASS NORMS

There are two systems of norms in our society. One, the middle class normative system, stresses an emphasis on achievement, work, responsibility, ambition, education, long-range goals, planning for the future, acquiring and maintaining property. Such values, if internalized, serve as an insulation against delinquent behavior.

Lower class norms, on the other hand, include a preoccupation with trouble, toughness, smartness, excitement, and a sense of fate. The ways of life in the lower class culture make these values just as reasonable or functional to lower class boys as middle class values are to the middle class way of life. The essential difference, however, is that these lower class values are conducive to crime and delinquency.

What Do You Think?

Review the theories described in this reading. What do you think are the most significant differences between these theories? Is there any combination of theories which you consider particularly enlightening? If we consider all of the theories as a whole, do they adequately explain the causes of crime? Why or why not? What other explanations would you add?

ACTIVITIES FOR INVOLVEMENT

1.   Review all of the readings in this chapter, as well as Chapter 2. What evidence can you find that could be used to *refute* each of these theories?

2.   Hold a mock newspaper interview in which a number of students are chosen to represent the individuals whose statements were quoted in the article entitled "Attitudes Toward Crime." Each student should be prepared to elaborate on his statement and to answer questions. The balance of the class might represent questioning reporters from a number of newspapers.

3.   How do you think Arthur Miller or Leonard Gross would respond to the individuals whose statements appear in the article entitled "Attitudes Toward Crime"? Write a short statement in which you attempt to express what you think they might say.

4.   The article by Gross entitled "Who Cares?" seems to stress the fact that many people today refuse to entangle themselves in the affairs of their fellows. Several explanations have been offered:

a. The increasing anonymity of our urban life. Very few people know many others on an intimate basis. It is not uncommon, for example, for apartment dwellers not to know who lives in the apartment next door to them.

b. Fear that involvement will mean a considerable intrusion on one's own privacy.

c. Being too busy with one's own affairs. Resentment at the possibility of inconvenience.

d. Basic dislike of other people.

e. An underlying fear that involvement means exposing oneself and one's weaknesses to others, with the resultant possibility that one will be emotionally hurt in the process.

f. Laziness.

g. Fear of physical harm.

Which of these, if any, do you think is the most adequate explanation for this lack of involvement? If you feel that none of these explanations are adequate, what explanation would you offer?

5.   One of the theories of crime which you read indicated that there is such a thing as a "criminal type." You often hear people remark that individuals represent one or another "type" of person. Listed below are several "types" which some educators have argued can be found in all groups. Would you agree?

    a. The brain.

    b. The athlete.

    c. The average guy.

    d. The "loner."

    e. The "leader."

    f. The "popularity kid."

Do each of these types exist in your class? Is it a good idea to type people? Why or why not?

6.   In 1965 a Harris poll asked why people become criminals. Their responses totaled as follows:

Cause	Per cent of Total Public
Upbringing	38
Bad environment	30
Mentally ill	16
Wrong companions	14
No education	14
Broken homes	13
Greed, easy money	13
Too much money around	11
Not enough money in home	10
Liquor, dope	10
Laziness	9
For kicks	8
No religion	8
No job	8
No chance by society	7
Born bad	5
Feeling of hopelessness	4
Moral breakdown of society	3
Degeneracy, sex	2
Failure of police	2

The percentages listed here total more than 100 since many respondents gave more than one answer. Which combination of the above do you feel would be most likely to contribute to a life of crime? Explain your reasoning.

7.   Look at Table I below. (a) What area of the country has the highest crime rate for personal crimes? For property crimes? Why do you suppose this is so? Can you offer any evidence to support your thinking? Where might you find such evidence? (b) Do you notice any trend as one moves away from the central city to the suburbs and out into rural areas? If so, describe what you detect.

TABLE I

REGIONAL AND COMMUNITY DIFFERENCES IN RATES OF SERIOUS CRIMES AGAINST THE PERSON AND CRIMES AGAINST PROPERTY

(Per 100,000 Population)

REGION	METROPOLITAN AREAS				NON-METROPOLITAN AREAS	
	Central Cities		Suburban Environs			
Northeast	Person:	513	Person:	293	Person:	62
	Property:	1,653	Property:	1,552	Property:	1,055
	N = (2,166)		N = (1,845)		N = (1,117)	
North Central	Person:	731	Person:	323	Person:	152
	Property:	2,780	Property:	1,533	Property:	1,010
	N = (3,511)		N = (1,856)		N = (1,162)	
South	Person:	315	Person:	536	Person:	120
	Property:	1,957	Property:	2,236	Property:	978
	N = (2,272)		N = (2,772)		N = (1,098)	
West	Person:	969	Person:	593	Person:	148
	Property:	3,204	Property:	2,579	Property:	2,224
	N = (4,173)		N = (3,172)		N = (2,372)	

SOURCE: NORC study, p. 29.

8.   Many people have argued that there is a relationship between race, income, and crime. Refer to Table IIA to evaluate this statement: "Negroes, no matter what their income group, are more likely to be victims of crime." In what ways do the statistics support or refute the statement?

Refer to Table IIB to evaluate this statement: "Whites are more likely to be victimized by Negroes than Negroes are by whites." In what ways do the statistics support or refute the statement?

Refer to Table III. What similarities and differences exist between Negro and white crime victims?

TABLE IIA

RACIAL AND INCOME DIFFERENCES IN RATES OF SERIOUS PERSONAL AND PROPERTY CRIMES

(Per 100,000 Population)

TYPE OF CRIME	INCOME UNDER $6,000		INCOME $6,000 OR MORE	
	Victim is White	Victim is Negro	Victim is White	Victim is Negro
Against person	402	748	244	262
Against property	1,829	1,927	1,765	3,024
N	(10,008)	(3,462)	(15,452)	(827)

SOURCE: NORC study, p. 32.

TABLE IIB
EXTENT OF INTERRACIAL CRIME

OFFENDER IS:	VICTIM IS:	
	White	Non-White
White	88%	19%
Non-White	12	81
Total	100%	100%
N	(705)	(118)

SOURCE: NORC study, p. 36.

TABLE III
MOST IMPORTANT REASON FOR NOT NOTIFYING POLICE BY RACE AND INCOME

REASON FOR NON-NOTIFICATION	WHITE		NON-WHITE	
	Under $6,000	$6,000 or More	Under $6,000	$6,000 or More
Not police concern	38%	30%	29%	25%
Fear of punishment	2	3	4	3
Personal refusal	9	9	20	9
Police would not be effective	51	58	47	63
Total	100%	100%	100%	100%
N	(265)	(455)	(79)	(32)

SOURCE: NORC study, p. 47.

How Should Police Deal with Crime?

5

One of the most controversial figures in existence today is the American police officer. Though he arouses a variety of emotions in people—hate, love, fear, respect, admiration—none would deny that his job is a difficult one. What should be the role of the police in dealing with crime and criminals? In this chapter, you will have the opportunity to read several articles which deal with that question.

1.   NEW PROBLEMS ON THE POLICE BEAT TODAY *

Policemen today have countless new problems and responsibilities that police officers a decade ago didn't even imagine. This article illustrates some of those problems.

Police Officer John E. Toomey, Badge Number 1261, walks a beat in North Beach.

He is tall and rugged, one of 1809 police officers who are covering 45 square miles of San Francisco day and night for the protection of an estimated 714,000 citizens.

Recently, at 9:17 P.M., at the intersection of Stockton and Union Streets near Washington Square, Officer Toomey observed what could have been the beginning of a car theft.

Suspicious, he approached the suspect, and began to ask questions of a dark-haired, chunky man in his mid-30's. A small group of passers-by gathered.

---

* Excerpted from Will Stevens, "New Problems on the Police Beat Today," San Francisco *Examiner,* October 1, 1967.

Down Stockton Street, less than half a block away, there was a cat-call. Then another. Then several. Officer Toomey continued his questioning.

TIMES CHANGE

Once upon a time, a check such as this would have been routine. No problems—and no catcalls. But times have changed. On a casual check such as this, one of many that evening, he was facing problems such as these—which all policemen are confronting around the clock:

At the scene of a potential arrest he swiftly had to evaluate: Was there a violation of the law? In this specific instance, it turned out well. There was no arrest. The questioning ended—and he moved on, ignoring the jeers police have learned to ignore these days.

ADDITIONAL PROBLEMS

Had there been a crime, however, and had Toomey determined he was going to make an actual arrest, he then would have been confronted with additional problems.

And these would have required swift answers after taking the circumstances into consideration:

What would be the consequences of his making the arrest? Would the individual submit, or would he resist and scream for those nearby to assist in fighting off an officer?

This was routine. But it could have been an actual arrest for anything ranging from aggravated assault to homicide—and a police arrest is being made every ten minutes in San Francisco.

NEW LAWS

Officer Toomey—like 1808 other San Francisco policemen—also has to know and understand the new and rigid decisions of the upper courts—*Massiah, Escobedo, Dorado, Anders, Gault* and others.

He must know and understand that an arrest case today may not end in Municipal Court. It may go all the way to the United States Supreme Court and possibly result in case law for police all over the country.

Indeed, the San Francisco policeman walking a beat or riding a radio car now must be a specialist: a veritable combined policeman-lawyer-judge-diplomat-psychologist.

Among other reasons, this is why there are 48 vacancies in the police department that have not been filled.

Today, for hundreds of officers often confronted with disrespect, new and difficult problems, and always a tremendous responsibility, it is not merely what they do but also how they do it that has become equally important.

GOT TO BE RIGHT

As Chief of Police Thomas J. Cahill points out:

They have countless new problems and responsibilities which police officers never had, even a decade ago.

"A suspect calling for help to fight off an officer happens often. It can result in a serious disturbance . . . a riot . . . or even the massive destruction of a city, as we [have seen in the past in many cities].

"You are asking a police officer to make decisions under the most difficult and challenging conditions . . . and he must make them swiftly. He's dealing with the liberty and perhaps the life of a person or persons, under circumstances such as this, and possibly even the tranquility of an entire city.

"Police officers today don't just have to be good. They've also got to be right."

ADDS TO PROBLEM

And yet—they are policemen, not lawyers. Sometimes they are wrong when they bring in a prisoner. And this becomes another factor in the alarming problem of overburdened court calendars, particularly in the municipal courts.

It's called turnstile justice.

The more cases tossed into the hopper—the more distorted becomes the rhythm of the judicial processes.

This does not mean that police are the prime cause. The prime cause is criminality itself . . . the kind that last year required police investigation in cases involving 49 homicides, 108 rapes, 2604 robberies, 2038 aggravated assaults, 11,719 burglaries, 8167 auto thefts, 3975 larceny cases—all felonies.

This did not include another 38,789 misdemeanor cases in which police made an arrest.

Another problem: the increasing necessity of officers to appear in court as witnesses in criminal cases.

Cahill describes this load as "fantastic," and nails it down with astonishing figures.

During last August, as a typical example, the court time of policemen totaled 2082 hours, or in excess of 260 man days with eight hours a normal shift.

Yet, as Cahill notes, "the increase in the number of our police officers is by no means sufficient."

What Do You Think?

San Francisco's Chief of Police, Thomas J. Cahill, states that today's police "don't just have to be good. They've also got to be right." What does he mean by this?

2.   ATTITUDES TOWARD THE POLICE *

How do different people feel about the police? How do you feel? What follows are the statements of several individuals—both civilians and police officers—concerning the police and their actions.

Some Citizens Speak

The following quotation is taken from a street interview with a lower class Negro youth:

(Q)   *What are your attitudes about the police? . . .*

(A)   I feel they are very belligerent people. They don't have no understanding of your problems. I mean, if you have a problem, they don't listen and try to understand you or nothing, man. Only thing, the police, you do what I say, that's the policeman.

(Q)   *Have you ever been stopped by the police?*

(A)   I been fighting the police.

(Q)   *How do you plan to fight them?*

(A)   With these, (pointing to hands) that's the only thing I got. And I'll keep on until they put me in jail. They put me in jail two or three times for fighting, and they'll put me in jail again if they mess with me again, the same way.

A white lawyer indicates the belief that the police particularly interrogate people who look different and whom the police think might be law violators:

* Excerpted from *The Police and the Community: The Dynamics of Their Relationship in a Changing Society,* Vols. I and II, *A Report Prepared for the President's Commission on Law Enforcement and Administration of Justice,* October, 1966. (Prepared under a grant by The Office of Law Enforcement Assistance, United States Department of Justice, to the University of California at Berkeley.)

"I've got a case right in my office right now that came in when it was thrown out the other day. A police officer stopped a Negro who was six foot four, and he was wearing a beard. He was driving his car down to the laundromat to do his laundry after he got off work. The officers stopped him; he asked them what for. One said, 'Well, I wanted to see how long your beard was. Let's see your driver's license.' There was no traffic offense, no mechanical violation. The policeman looks at his driver's license, and says, 'I'm going to call in and see if there is anything out for you.' He calls in and there is a warrant with the same name, a traffic warrant . . . failure to appear. They go to the Marshal's Office, this guy is begging them to check the license number on that other citation, check the description. He has to go to the Marshal's office where this information is kept, refuses to check it, takes him in, makes him bail out. Comes to court, they find out that they were looking for a five foot six, 140 pound, blond, blue-eyed Caucasian."

A white youth speaks:

"Well, I've noticed that they've been pretty petty, picayunish. A prime example—I was hitchhiking to work at 7:15 in the morning, which isn't unreasonable, and I was down in Pacific Beach, and I was standing there hitchhiking and was dressed neatly to go to work, and a policeman came on over, wants to know what I'm doing. And naturally I told him I'm hitchhiking to work, and I got twenty minutes to make it all the way down in San Diego. And I'd appreciate it if he could just, you know, go along and take care of somebody else, because I'm not breaking any laws and I want to get to work. He says, 'No, I can't do that; I've got to know everybody that's on my beat.' And so he proceeded to check my identification, where I lived and what not, what I did for an occupation. And this took ten to fifteen minutes. Finally I persuaded him . . . to take off so I could get to work, and he says, 'Well, I'm sorry to keep you delayed all this time. I've got to know who is in my area, district, and what to look out for,' and all this. And I didn't appreciate it, because I ended up being about twenty minutes late for work, and my employer didn't appreciate it."

Other youths comment with regards to the officers' honesty.

"On Friday night, if a cop catch you and you do something, if you have a little money on you, you can pay it and they'll let you . . . they'll ride you around the block and let you off. But if you ain't got no money, they will whip the hell out of you and take you down to the station."

A Negro youth expresses himself concerning the Negro officer:

"They ain't no good. See, what it is—the Negro cop . . . 'cause they got a little suit on, they think they're better than us. Average time you might get the red car, colored and white man in there, the white cop, he'll let you go; the old colored cop, he beat you up. Just sometimes it's the reverse; average time, though, it's the colored cop, 'cause he figures he's better than anyone else."

Another personalized his response:

"Cause I know from experience, two police . . . sometime the colored . . . you know, like we be in a gang or something, we don't exactly be going nowhere to fight or nothing, we be coming from a party, there's a lot of us. And the cop, you know, he just say, 'All right,' you know, 'have no trouble, go ahead home.' But a colored cop—he'll jump out, you know, stop you and everything, and push you around. The police . . . the colored police, you know, they'll be trying to work harder than some of the white."

The same youth explained the cause for the Negro officer's behavior: "Sometimes he's trying to make an impression on a white cop." Generally the sentiment was in favor of the Negro officer when alone. One youth explained:

"Yeah. See, when . . . like a police officer's by himself, you know, he won't mess with you; but two or three of them, you know,—that's when they get all bad, you know, and they want to whup you up."

A Mexican-American clergyman in San Diego, California:

"You can't straighten them [the police] out by running them through the Police Academy and exposing them to a few hours of lectures on human relations and the equality and dignity of the races. You know that all his life he [the policeman] has been taught that equality and dignity of the individual has primary reference to the white individual, and that the individual of the minority group is not really part of humanity in the broad sense. He [the minority person] is sub human, in a sub culture."

The Police Present Their Side

A community liaison officer meets with various groups in the community:

"He makes an effort to convey to his civilian audiences what he be-lieves is the special situation and circumstances of the policeman. He describes the side of life with which the policeman often deals:

'In one day I have seen, I have arrested a man for robbery—a crim-inal. I have gone into a house and lying in bed was a child, dead, and dead for several hours, and the mother doesn't even know it; the diaper on that kid has never been changed, it looks like weeks, just peel it off. Terrible! I have had a call for a suicide, walk into a room as a man has stuck a shotgun in his mouth, and pulled the trigger. And then I have had to go out and make a contact with a person who feels like yourself.' "

According to the Lieutenant, it is often necessary for a policeman to use force if he is to do his job. He adds that much of the outcry about police brutality stems from ambiguous definitions of what constitutes nec-essary force. The head of the Community Liaison Unit adds:

"Now, I would not insult your intelligence. We have 750 policemen; everyone is not perfect. Every man does not react in a proper profes-sional manner under all circumstances; each policeman is a human being and mistakes will be made. But in our city we think the key to it is this; when an act of misconduct or brutality comes to our attention we do something about it. That policeman is reprimanded, suspended, or fired, depending upon the circumstances. We don't whitewash him, we don't throw him under the carpet; we do something."

The Community Liaison Officer defends the Department's practice of field interrogations as a necessary tool to combat crime.

"Why are teenagers stopped and questioned at all times during the day? Of course there has to be a reason for it. The policeman is suspi-cious because of the area, of the time of day, of what the person is doing, and because crimes for the area have been occurring in which the per-son stopped fits the general description. He stops to investigate. The key to this, and you just can't stop someone arbitrarily, is that the average person who is stopped is stopped with reasonable cause. Would the average person who observed this particular situation that that policeman observed have come to the same conclusion that that policeman came to, based upon what he saw? And that's the criteria. We feel it is up to the Police Department to make each one of these field interrogations a public relations contact, and the way to do that is simple—justify each stop in the mind of the person that you are stopping. We have found that when the field interrogations go down in any area of our city, the burglaries and robberies go up just like clockwork. When the field interrogations come up, the burglaries and robberies go down. I can show you this over the past fifteen years, just like that."

The Police Department professes that it makes an effort to gain the support and understanding of juveniles in the community and to mitigate their hostility. The Community Liaison Officer explains the nature of their effort as follows:

"We tell these kids, we tell each one of them, 'If a policeman stops you and if he's mean or he's a bully . . . we want you to go to your parents and we want your parents to call the station. And we'll do something about it.' Because each policeman must treat this youngster as a lady or a gentleman. But this is a two-way street. That policeman stops you on the street and your first reaction is, 'Look, Cop, don't bug me; I'm busy,' then he might not be as tactful as he should be. So we tell these kids that this is the way to look at it. . . . To improve their attitude. What do we do? Let's say a policeman stops a youngster for a routine field interrogation and he stops this kid and his attitude is poor. The kid starts off with 'Look, Cop, don't bug me; I'm busy,' or some other nice colloquialism. What do we do? Well, we make out a little slip and send it to the Juvenile Division and the next day one of our Detectives goes to the home and talks to the parents and the kid at the same time and tries to find out why this youngster feels this way and to work out whatever they can to alleviate the attitude on the part of this person. And this, again, has conclusively shown itself to be successful."

A Philadelphia police officer presents another perspective:

"When you drive up, you're a cop . . . you represent authority. Maybe some other policeman in the same car, on the same shift last night, hit somebody. You—it's automatically assumed that you're going to hit somebody. You may be the nicest guy in the world. So you've got a hostile group of people to start out with. Now, how do you play it? So one guy puts his hands in his pocket. You gonna stop and rationalize now? Some guy's putting his hand in his pocket to scratch his leg, or is he looking for his knife?"

The Deputy Sheriff of Multnomah County (Portland, Oregon) recently wrote a letter to the editor of the *New Republic* in which he said: "It seems unfair to me that the police are the goats for a few hundred years of racial oppression. Let the journalists, the milkmen, or any other group of workers handle the next race riot and see how popular they are with the Negroes after it's over. We do not make the laws, we only enforce them." [1]

A social action official comments on the Negro officer:

"It would depend on this. I think . . . very often, the Negroes resent the Negro patrolman too, because he is viewed as the *sellout,* he has become the sellout. So, you know you are damned if you do, and damned if you don't. I mean, none of these things is easy. . . ."

And, lastly, a Negro officer in Philadelphia comments:

"Well, let me remind you that you're on unsafe ground when you criticize policies and practices of your own Department. However, I do feel that, if policemen are ever going to project this kind of image that should be projected, and if we are going to ever develop a real understanding between the community and the Police Department, I think we all must search our own conscience and we must discuss these things as we see them.

"I kind of believe that policemen have to be a protector of law and somewhat of a social worker also, if they are really going to be that real buffer between the administration and the community.

"And I just presently cannot see all of this coming from the Police Department itself. I believe some of it is going to have to come from without. I believe the Federal Government is going to have to step in, with the cities, and come forward with consultants and specialists, that they can move into communities and help the Police Department get on the right road to understanding what the real problems of the community are today. . . .

"I also feel that . . . the Police Department with this Community Relations program ought to develop the kind of training whereby it will erase, or attempt to erase, from the policemen's minds that policemen are disliked by the entire community. And I think the Police Departments are making a real mistake by ignoring this, because when a person feels that he is disliked, I think too often he goes out into the community with a chip on his shoulder feeling that he is disliked. And I believe when people have this kind of feeling, it causes them to be in an awkward position in trying to function fairly."

---

[1] Excerpted from James R. Piland, "Policing the Police: A Reply," *The New Republic,* October 16, 1965.

What Do You Think?

1. Compare the various views expressed in this reading by civilians and police. What similarities and differences do you notice? How would you explain these similarities and differences?
2. How would you reply to the deputy sheriff's statement that the police do not make the laws, they only enforce them?

3. POLICE AUTHORITY AND PRACTICES *

What things may a police officer legally do in order to carry out his job?

The policeman's lot is indeed a difficult one. He is charged with applying and enforcing a multitude of laws and ordinances in a degree or proportion and in a manner that maintain a delicate balance between the liberty of the individual and a high degree of social protection. . . . He must enforce the law, yet he must also determine whether a particular violation should be handled by warning or arrest. He is not expected to arrest every violator. Some laws were never intended by the enactors to be enforced, and others condemn behavior that is not contrary to significant moral values. If he arrested all the violators, the courts would find it impossible to do their work, and he would be in court so frequently that he could not perform his other professional duties. Consequently, the policeman must judge and informally settle more cases than he takes to court. . . .

Even if total enforcement were possible, constitutional, statutory, and judicial limitations upon police procedures would preclude it. . . .

WARRANTS

An arrest is the taking into custody of a person so that he may be held to answer for the commission of a crime. It may be either with or without a warrant. If the arrest is by warrant, the process is started by a complaining witness appearing before a magistrate and making a written statement under oath of essential facts constituting the offense charged and requesting the issuance of a warrant for the arrest of the accused. . . .

If the magistrate finds from the complaint "probable cause" to be-

* Excerpted from Richard C. Donnelly, "Police Authority and Practices," *Annals of the American Academy of Political and Social Science*, CCCXXXIX, January, 1962.

lieve that an offense has been committed and that the accused committed it, a warrant is issued.

The vast majority of arrests, however, are made without a warrant. The limits of lawful arrest without a warrant vary considerably in different jurisdictions. . . . In the case of a felony, the situation is broadly as follows:

    a. An officer may arrest when a felony has actually been committed or is in the process of being committed and the person arrested committed the crime;

    b. An officer may arrest when a felony has actually been committed and he has reasonable grounds to believe that the person arrested committed it even though in fact he did not;

    c. An officer may arrest when a felony has not been committed but he nonetheless has reasonable grounds to believe that one has been committed and that the person arrested did the act.

In the case of a misdemeanor, there was no power at common law to arrest for a misdemeanor without a warrant unless the misdemeanor constituted a breach of the peace and was committed in the officer's presence. However, many states have now extended the power of arrest without warrant to all misdemeanors committed in the officer's presence. . . .

APPEARANCE BEFORE MAGISTRATE

Once a person has been arrested, the Federal Rules of Criminal Procedure require that he be taken "without unnecessary delay" before the nearest available magistrate. Similar provisions exist in the states. What happens after presentation to the magistrate will depend upon the seriousness of the offense charged. If the charge is for a minor or petty offense the magistrate may have the power and authority to try the case himself. If so, he will usually proceed with the trial, unless the accused is entitled to a jury trial and requests it or unless a continuance is granted. If the offense charged is a felony or serious misdemeanor, the magistrate will ordinarily lack the authority to conduct a trial but will hold a preliminary hearing. Although a relatively informal proceeding, the accused is entitled to an attorney, he may cross-examine witnesses against him, and he may introduce evidence in his own behalf. Under the federal practice, he must be informed that he is not required to make a statement but, if he does, the statement may be used against him. If the magistrate finds from the evidence probable cause that an offense has been committed and that the accused committed it, the latter is bound over to await the action of the grand jury or of the prosecuting attorney in jurisdictions where indictment by grand jury is no longer required.

Police practice departs markedly from these rules of arrest. Arrests on suspicion alone, arrests without presentation before a magistrate, and roundups of individuals with prior arrest records are common. These arrests are clearly illegal under existing law. Often persons are charged with disorderly conduct or vagrancy as a subterfuge for holding them when there is insufficient evidence to support a more serious offense.

USE OF FORCE

How much force is an officer permitted to use in order to accomplish a lawful arrest? Although generalizations are again dangerous, the general rule . . . is that an officer may use all the force that is reasonably necessary to make a lawful arrest, with or without warrant, and no more. The issue here is whether he may use deadly force when it is not necessary for self-protection or for the protection of another but only to effect arrest. The common law was based on the distinction between felony and misdemeanor—deadly force being authorized when necessary to prevent the escape of one fleeing from arrest for felony, but not for a misdemeanor.

This distinction is inadequate for modern law. The rational justification for the common law rests largely on the fact that virtually all felonies in the common law period were punishable by death. Today, relatively few crimes are punishable by death. Moreover, some statutory misdemeanors, such as reckless driving, involve conduct more dangerous than some felonies. . . .

A police officer may be under a duty to perform an official act inside a house or building. For instance, he may hold a warrant to arrest someone who is in a house, or he may have reasonable grounds for believing a felony is being committed inside. Under these circumstances, if he first states his authority and purpose for demanding admission and is then denied entrance, he may break his way in. . . .

SEARCH AND SEIZURES

The Fourth Amendment to the United States Constitution forbids "unreasonable searches and seizures" and provides that "no warrants shall issue, but upon probable cause." Similar guarantees are embodied in the various state constitutions or in acts of the legislatures. These provisions are general in their terms, and the courts, with very little additional guidance, must determine what is unreasonable and what is reasonable.

A search is reasonable when it is made in accordance with the terms of a search warrant issued by a magistrate on the basis of affidavits containing these three essential elements: (1) A statement of facts showing probable cause that a crime has been committed; (2) A specification of the place or places to be searched; and (3) A description, with reasonable particularity, of the articles sought. Ordinarily, the search must be made in the daytime and within a stated time from its issuance—within ten days in the federal system. . . .

Although the Fourth Amendment and similar state provisions do not say that a warrant must be used for all searches, this view could reasonably be implied. Nevertheless, the courts have interpreted the provisions as not requiring a search warrant when the search is incidental to a lawful arrest, where the object of the search is a movable vehicle, or when the accused has consented to the search, thereby waiving his constitutional protection.

SEARCH WITHOUT WARRANT

When the search is based upon consent, questions frequently arise as to whom (*sic*) may give consent and whether consent was in fact given. The burden of proving the latter is upon the prosecution. . . . Furthermore, the absence of duress or coercion must also be affirmatively shown by the prosecution. . . .

Another exception to the rule that a search cannot be conducted without a warrant occurs when the object of the search is an automobile, boat, motorcycle, or other vehicle that can be quickly moved out of the jurisdiction in which the warrant would have to be obtained. Mobility creates a special situation which justifies a search upon probable cause without a warrant.

Search without a warrant is permissible when incidental to a lawful arrest. . . . The search . . . must remain within proper limits; that is, it must be truly "incidental." This problem of setting bounds presents many troublesome questions. It is clear that the arresting officer may search the prisoner and the immediate vicinity for weapons and instruments that might aid escape. In addition, he is allowed to make some search for the purpose of guarding the proceeds of crime, contraband, and important material evidence from loss or destruction. Whether the officer may go beyond this and, if so, how far, is left in doubt by the cases. Some are unduly liberal and some unduly restrictive. Probably the most extreme case decided by the Supreme Court of the United States was *Harris v. United States,* where a majority of five to four held that an incidental search might extend to an entire five-room apartment even though the defendant was arrested in the living room.

WIRE TAPPING AND EAVESDROPPING

Related to search and seizures is the problem presented by wire tapping and other forms of electronic eavesdropping such as concealed microphones. Technologically, a vast breakthrough has occurred in eavesdropping techniques. Parabolic microphones are available that can beam in on conversations from hundreds of yards away; resonator radio transmitters the size of match boxes can be planted under a table or bed to send conversations to receiving sets a mile away; telephone tap connections no longer need to be made by crude splicing of wires but can be done by refined induction coil devices; tape recorders small enough to fit into a coat pocket have been invented, as have "television eyes" small enough to be hidden in a heating duct or light fixtures; and tiny automatic cameras are able to photograph almost in the dark with infra-red film. All of these devices are used by the police.

Wire tapping is . . . only a specialized form of eavesdropping, and the federal statute as well as most state statutes are limited to the former. Whether there is a search and seizure when other electronic devices or means are used depends upon whether there has been a trespass. In *On Lee v. United States,* an informer had entered On Lee's laundry and engaged him in conversation. Unbeknown to On Lee, there was a small radio transmitter concealed upon the informer which broadcast their discussion to a government agent some distance away. No recording was made of the conversation, but the agent was allowed to testify as to the contents of the purported conversation. The majority of the Court held this was not an unreasonable search or seizure although strong dissents on various grounds were filed by four members of the Court.

In *Silverman v. United States,* however, a "spike mike" was used. This instrument consisted of a microphone with a spike attached to it, together with an amplifier, a power pack, and earphones. The spike was driven into a wall until it made contact with a heating duct, which converted the entire heating system into a conductor of sound. The Supreme Court unanimously held this conduct to be a violation of the Fourth Amendment.

INFORMERS

A closely allied practice in the detection of crime is the use of police informers and undercover agents. They are widely used by police departments and law enforcement agencies. . . . Indeed, a former United States Attorney estimates that 95 per cent of all federal narcotics cases are obtained as a result of the work of informers, whether they be paid or not.

In order to protect and maintain the sources of information given by informers, the courts have developed the "informer's privilege," which is in fact the government's privilege to keep the name of the informer secret. . . .

INTERROGATION OF SUSPECTS

Although the police are permitted to question suspects, they must observe certain civilities. First, and most important, the questioning must not be "coercive" or too intimidating. While the police may use methods of interrogation involving trickery, fabricated evidence, subtle threats, and violations of confidence, they must stop short of "coercion." If "third degree" methods . . . are employed, the resulting admissions or confessions are usually inadmissible at the trial. Second, the questioning must not interfere with or delay the progress of the arrest. As mentioned above, the arrested person must be taken promptly before a magistrate for a preliminary hearing. The interrogation may not legally impede this. Third, the suspect is under no obligation to talk or answer questions at all, and anything done or said by an officer to make him feel that he is under such an obligation is stepping out of bounds.

What Do You Think?

1. What evidence does Donnelly present to support his statement that "the policeman's lot is indeed a difficult one"?
2. Should any of the limitations now placed on the police which Donnelly describes be removed? Explain your answer.
3. Should police be allowed to use "almost any means" in order to make an important arrest? What is an "important arrest"? When, if ever, should police be allowed to use violence? Explain your answers.

4. VIOLENCE AND THE POLICE *

When may a policeman resort to violence in the performance of his duties? In this article, we see how the police feel about this question.

The policeman finds his most pressing problems in his relationships to the public. His is a service occupation but of an incongruous kind, since he must discipline those whom he serves. He is regarded as corrupt and inefficient by, and meets with hostility and criticism from, the public. He regards the public as his enemy, feels his occupation to be in conflict with the community. The experience and the feeling give rise to a collective emphasis on secrecy, an attempt to coerce respect from the public, and a belief that almost any means are legitimate in completing an important arrest. These are for the policeman basic occupational values. They arise from his experience, take precedence over his legal responsibilities, are central to an understanding of his conduct, and form the occupational contexts within which violence gains its meaning. . . .

DUTY AND VIOLENCE

In the United States the use of violence by the police is both an occupational prerogative and a necessity. . . .

---

* Excerpted from William A. Westley, "Violence and the Police," *American Journal of Sociology,* LIX, July, 1953.

The armed criminal who has demonstrated a casual regard for the lives of others and a general hatred of the policeman forces the use of violence by the police in the pursuit of duty. Every policeman has some such experiences, and they proliferate in police lore.

The apprehension and conviction of the felon is, for the policeman, the essence of police work. It is the source of prestige both within and outside police circles, it has career implications, and it is a major source of justification for the existence of the police before a critical and often hostile public. Out of these conditions a legitimation for the illegal use of violence is wrought.

Seventy-three policemen, drawn from all ranks and constituting approximately 50 per cent of the patrolmen, were asked, "When do you think a policeman is justified in roughing a man up?" . . .

Examples of some of the responses . . . that fall into the "disrespect for the police" category follow:

"Well, there are cases. For example, when you stop a fellow for a routine questioning, say a wise guy, and he starts talking back to you and telling you you are no good and that sort of thing. You know you can take a man in on a disorderly conduct charge, but you can practically never make it stick. So what you do in a case like that is to egg the guy on until he makes a remark where you can justifiably slap him and, then, if he fights back, you can call it resisting arrest."

"Well, it varies in different cases. Most of the police use punishment if the fellow gives them any trouble. Usually you can judge a man who will give you trouble though. *If there is any slight resistance,* you can go all out on him. You shouldn't do it in the street, though. Wait until you are in the squad car, because, even if you are in the right and a guy takes a poke at you, just when you are hitting back somebody's just likely to come around the corner, and what he will say is that you are beating the guy with your club."

"Well, a prisoner deserves to be hit when he goes to the point where he tries to put you below him.

"You gotta get rough when a man's language becomes very bad, when he is trying to make a fool of you in front of everybody else. I think most policemen try to treat people in a nice way, but usually you have to talk pretty rough. That's the only way to set a man down, to make him show a little respect."

THE USE OF VIOLENCE

The sanctions for the use of violence . . . and the fact that policemen morally justify even its illegal use may suggest that violence is employed with great frequency and little provocation. Such an impression would be erroneous, for the actual use of violence is limited by other considerations, such as individual inclinations, the threat of detection, and a sensitivity to public reactions.

All policemen, however, are conscious of the dangers of the illegal use of violence. If detected, they may be subject to a lawsuit and possibly dismissal from the force. Therefore, they limit its use to what they think they can get away with. . . .

However, different portions of the public have differing definitions of conduct and are of differential importance to the policeman, and the way in which the police define different portions of the public has an effect on whether or not they will use violence.

The police believe that certain groups of persons will respond only to fear and rough treatment. In the city studied they defined both Negroes and slum dwellers in this category. The following statements . . . typify the manner in which they discriminate the public:

"In the good districts you appeal to people's judgment and explain the law to them. In the South Side the only way is to appear like you are the boss.

"You can't ask them a question and get an answer that is not a lie. In the South Side the only way to walk into a tavern is to walk in swaggering as if you own the place and if somebody is standing in your way give him an elbow and push him aside.

"The colored people understand one thing. The policeman is the law, and he is going to treat you rough and that's the way you have to treat them. Personally, I don't think the colored are trying to help themselves one bit. If you don't treat them rough, they will sit right on top of your head."

Discriminations with respect to the public are largely based on the political power of the group, the degree to which the police believe that the group is potentially criminal, and the type of treatment which the police believe will elicit respect from it.

What Do You Think?

1. Would you refute Westley's statement that the use of violence by the police is a necessity? Why or why not?
2. Are most people inclined to be respectful or disrespectful of police? Explain. What factors in our society might produce such an attitude?
3. How would you explain the fact that many individual policemen who themselves condemn the use of violence still will not openly condemn their fellows for such acts?

5. "THEY VIEW THE LAW WITH CONTEMPT AND THE POLICE WITH DISTRUST" *

Lastly, here is a brief statement of a new kind of relationship which the author thinks may be developing between the citizenry and the police. What do you think?

American law enforcement procedures have never been designed to control large groups of citizens in rebellion, but to protect the social structure against specifically criminal acts, or persons. The underlying assumption has always been that the police and the citizenry form a national alliance against evil and dangerous crooks, who should certainly be arrested on sight and shot if they resist.

There are indications, however, that this "natural alliance" might be going the way of the Maginot Line (a supposedly impregnable defense which the French constructed during World War I, but which detained the invading Germans only a few days). More and more often the police are finding themselves in conflict with whole blocs of the citizenry, none of them criminals in the traditional sense of the word, but many as potentially dangerous—to the police—as any armed felon. This is particularly true in situations involving groups of Negroes and teenagers. The Watts riot in Los Angeles in 1965 was a classic example of this new alignment. A whole community turned on the police with such a vengeance that the National Guard had to be called in. Yet few of the rioters were criminals—at least not until the riot began. It may be that America is developing a whole new category of essentially social criminals . . . persons who threaten the police and the traditional social structure, even when they are breaking no law . . . because they view The Law with contempt and the police with distrust, and this abiding resentment can explode without warning at the slightest provocation.

What Do You Think?

1.   What evidence can you offer to support or refute Thompson's thesis?
2.   If the relationship between the citizenry and the police is actually developing as Thompson suggests, what implications might this have for American society as a whole?

---

* Excerpted from Hunter S. Thompson, *Hell's Angels: A Strange and Terrible Saga,* New York, N. Y.: Random House, 1967.

ACTIVITIES FOR INVOLVEMENT

1. Invite a policeman from your community to speak to the class on the problems which policemen face today. Present him with a number of the arguments or statements found in the readings in this chapter and ask him to comment. Would he recommend police work as a career?

2. Look up the decisions made by the courts in the *Massiah, Escobedo, Dorado, Anders,* and *Gault* cases. What restrictions have these decisions placed on the police? Invite a lawyer and a police official to discuss the implications of these decisions for the police with the class.

3. Invite some members of the local community (e.g., a housewife, a city official, a high school dropout, a member of a civil rights group, etc.) to express their views on the role of the police in modern society. Prepare questions (like the following) to ask the speakers:
   a. What qualities should policemen possess?
   b. What kind of training would you recommend for police officers?
   c. What limitations or restrictions should be placed on police actions? Why?

Compare their responses and reactions with those of the policeman you invited.

4. Listed below are a number of qualifications which various people have suggested police officers should possess. Pick the five you think are most important and the five which you think are least important. Explain your choices. Would you add or substitute any qualifications besides those listed?

intelligent	healthy	charming
brave	young	handsome
big	quick	religious
physically strong	cautious	simple in his tastes
patient	subtle	not married
stubborn	tactful	politically neutral
calm	friendly	lower class socioeconomically
friendly	suspicious	from a minority racial or
emotionally stable	have college degree	ethnic group
		honest

Compare your selections with those of your classmates and then try to come to some decision as to what the "ideal policeman" should be like. What problems arise in trying to arrive at a decision?

5. How much force should a police officer be permitted to use in order to make a lawful arrest? The general rule, according to Donnelly, is that an officer may use "all the force that is reasonably necessary." The question, of course, is what is meant by "reasonably necessary." How would you define the term? Would you consider any of the following to be "reasonably necessary" for force to be used?
   a. Whenever disrespect for the police is shown.
   b. Whenever force is impossible to avoid.

   c. To obtain information from an individual.

   d. To make an arrest.

   e. Whenever dealing with a "hardened" criminal.

   f. When the officer knows the individual is guilty.

Explain the reasoning behind your selections.

   6.   A second, and just as important, question is who should decide what is reasonably necessary. To which of the following individuals or groups would you be willing to grant this power?

   a. The policeman himself.

   b. A judge.

   c. An elected city official.

   d. An appointed city official.

   e. A group of professional educators.

   f. A group of average people chosen at random from the community.

   g. A board of police officials.

   h. A mixed group of church officials from a variety of faiths.

Rank these individuals from (1), lowest, to (8), highest, and then explain why you ranked them as you did. Compare your rankings with those of your classmates.

   7.   Look at Table IVA. (a) What variations in the risk of victimization for different types of crime do you notice among different income levels in the population? By race? By age and sex? (b) Do the statistics in these tables support or refute the argument that people with certain characteristics are more likely than others to be victims of crime? (c) If the general public were made aware of statistics like those in Tables IVA through C, might this help efforts to control and prevent crimes? Explain.

TABLE IVA
VICTIMIZATION BY INCOME

(Rates per 100,000 population)

OFFENSES	INCOME			
	$0 to $2,999	$3,000 to $5,999	$6,000 to $9,999	Above $10,000
Total	2,369	2,331	1,820	2,237
Forcible rape	76	49	10	17
Robbery	172	121	48	34
Aggravated assault	229	316	144	252
Burglary	1,319	1,020	867	790
Larceny ($50 and over)	420	619	549	925
Motor vehicle theft	153	206	202	219
Number of respondents	(5,232)	(8,238)	(10,382)	(5,946)

SOURCE: Philip H. Ennis, "Criminal Victimization in the United States: A Report of a National Survey." Field Survey II, President's Commission on Law Enforcement and Administration of Justice. (Washington: U.S. Government Printing Office, 1967), adapted from table 14, p. 31.

TABLE IVB
VICTIMIZATION BY RACE

(Rates per 100,000 population)

OFFENSES	WHITE	NON-WHITE
Total	1,860	2,592
Forcible rape	22	82
Robbery	58	204
Aggravated assault	186	347
Burglary	822	1,306
Larceny ($50 and over)	608	367
Motor vehicle theft	164	286
Number of respondents	(27,484)	(4,902)

SOURCE: NORC study, adapted from table 16, p. 33.

TABLE IVC
VICTIMIZATION BY AGE AND SEX

(Rates per 100,000 population)

OFFENSE	MALE						
	10–19	20–29	30–39	40–49	50–59	60 plus	All ages
Total	951	5,924	6,231	5,150	4,231	3,465	3,091
Robbery	61	257	112	210	181	98	112
Aggravated assault	399	824	337	263	181	146	287
Burglary	123	2,782	3,649	2,365	2,297	2,343	1,583
Larceny ($50 and over)	337	1,546	1,628	1,839	967	683	841
Motor vehicle theft	31	515	505	473	605	195	268
	FEMALE						
Total	334	2,424	1,514	1,908	1,132	1,052	1,059
Forcible rape	91	238	104	48	0	0	83
Robbery	0	238	157	96	60	81	77
Aggravated assault	91	333	52	286	119	40	118
Burglary	30	665	574	524	298	445	314
Larceny ($50 and over)	122	570	470	620	536	405	337
Motor vechile theft	0	380	157	334	119	81	130

SOURCE: NORC study, adapted from table 17, pp. 34–35.

8.   Read the "Law Enforcement Code of Ethics" which follows below. This oath is taken by all newly appointed police officers. Some individuals have said that this is too much to expect of policemen who are, after all,

as human as the rest of us. How would you react to this statement? Explain your reasoning.

LAW ENFORCEMENT CODE OF ETHICS

As a law enforcement officer, my fundamental duty is to serve mankind; to safeguard lives and property; to protect the innocent against deception, the weak against oppression or intimidation, and the peaceful against violence or disorder; and to respect the Constitutional rights of all men to liberty, equality, and justice.

I will keep my private life unsullied as an example to all; maintain courageous calm in the face of danger, scorn, or ridicule; develop self-restraint; and be constantly mindful of the welfare of others. Honest in thought and deed in both my personal and official life, I will be exemplary in obeying the laws of the land and the regulations of my department. Whatever I see or hear of a confidential nature or that is confided to me in my official capacity will be kept ever secret unless revelation is necessary in the performance of my duty.

I will never act officiously or permit personal feelings, prejudices, animosities, or friendships to influence my decisions. With no compromise for crime and with relentless prosecution of criminals, I will enforce the law courteously and appropriately without fear or favor, malice, or ill will, never employing unnecessary force or violence and never accepting gratuities.

I recognize the badge of my office as a symbol of public faith, and I accept it as a public trust to be held so long as I am true to the ethics of the police service. I will constantly strive to achieve these objectives and ideals, dedicating myself before God to my chosen profession—law enforcement.

Can Crime
Be Eliminated?

Can we eliminate, or at least substantially reduce, crime in the United States? And if so, what steps should we take? Some people urge harsh punishment, the building of more jails, and the hiring of more police; others place an emphasis on rehabilitation and stress the need for more psychiatrists, psychologists, and social workers. A few say that there can never be enough police or prisons—that the answer lies in men's hearts. Before we can begin to get rid of crime, man himself must change.

Today some people think that the weights of justice have been tipped too far in favor of the criminal—at the expense of public safety. In particular, critics point to several United States Supreme Court decisions of the past decade which they say are allowing too many criminals literally to get away with murder. Among the Court rulings most often criticized are:

Mallory v. U. S. (1957), in which the Supreme Court invalidated a defendant's confession because arresting officers failed to bring the suspect before a judge "without reasonable delay."

Mapp v. Ohio (1961), in which the Court ruled that state courts could not accept evidence that had been obtained in violation of the "reasonable search clause" of the Fourth Amendment. In practice this meant that law enforcement agencies in many states had to obtain search warrants for the first time in their experience.

Escobedo v. Illinois (1964), in which the Court invalidated the state conviction of Danny Escobedo on a murder charge. Reason: the police refused to let Escobedo see his lawyer (who was waiting in the next room) before he confessed to the crime. The ruling hinted that a suspect's Constitutional right to counsel begins as soon as the police focus on him as a prime suspect. Since this

83

is precisely the point at which most confessions are sought, the decision threw police around the country into turmoil. For the first advice most lawyers give to clients is to say nothing. Hence, no confession.

In this chapter you will read a number of arguments concerning how society should deal with those who engage in criminal behavior. As you read, weigh the opposing philosophies and the practical methods used to implement them. Which methods, if any, would you endorse?

1. IS THE U. S. CODDLING CRIMINALS? *

Have rulings such as those discussed above given rights to criminals at the expense of public safety? Here are arguments on both sides of the question.

Yes!

1. *Recent Court decisions in effect encourage criminal acts.*

According to statistics released by the Federal Bureau of Investigation (FBI), crime is rising at an alarming rate in the U. S.—more than six times the rate of population growth. Yet the Supreme Court seems to be more interested in protecting criminals than in protecting the safety of law-abiding citizens.

Take the 1966 *Miranda* decision, for instance. The Court reversed the convictions of four men who in detailed confessions *admitted* to crimes of robbery, rape, and murder. The men walked away free because they did not have access to lawyers during the time they were first interrogated by police officers. The question of guilt or innocence was totally ignored by the Justices. The victims of these brutal crimes were not taken into consideration. The Court ruled that these four men were treated "unjustly" because they were denied their "rights."

This is dangerous for the population as a whole. By freeing criminals the Court encourages more crime in the nation. FBI chief J. Edgar Hoover calls this the "tragedy of soft justice."

The Bill of Rights is essential to our democracy. But it must not be used to undermine the right of individuals to be *protected* from crime.

---

* "Is the U. S. Coddling Criminals?" *Senior Scholastic,* Vol. 90, No. 3, February 17, 1967. By permission *Senior Scholastic,* © 1967 Scholastic Magazines, Inc.

2. *Supreme Court decisions have handcuffed the police in the performance of their duties.*

Many legal experts doubt that law-enforcement agencies now have the legal weapons needed to check rising violence, theft, and organized crime. For the pendulum has swung too far toward the protection of the individual criminal and too far away from the protection of society.

Inducing or tricking confessions out of suspects has long been one of the most effective devices for solving difficult crimes. As former Deputy Police Commissioner of New York City, Richard Dougherty, puts it: "The truth is that most crimes are not solved by fingerprints and wristwatch radios, or the skillful assembling of clues. The suspect confesses." Yet recent decisions by the Supreme Court seem to ignore this basic fact and work to handcuff the police and thus prevent them from doing an effective job.

For example, two days after the brutal slaying of eight student nurses in Chicago recently, police arrested the prime suspect—Richard Speck. Three days later Speck still had not been questioned by the authorities. Why? Police feared that if they failed to dot all the legal "i's" during any interrogation period, Speck's remarks would not be allowed as evidence at his trial.

Certainly the legal rights of every citizen must be guaranteed, but not to such extremes that they jeopardize the safety of other citizens. The Court itself has ruled that the right of free speech does not permit someone to falsely shout "fire" in a crowded theatre and thus cause a panic. Similarly, a suspect's right should not be an excuse for permitting criminals to jeopardize public safety.

3. *The U. S. needs a tougher approach to crime and punishment.*

Strict laws enforced by a strong police system are the best medicine to cure any crime epidemic. There has rarely been a period in history when we needed to get tougher with criminals and end what Roman Catholic Bishop Fulton J. Sheen calls "false compassion" for criminals.

There has already been a loud public reaction to the "turn 'em loose" attitude of the Supreme Court. Responsible citizens around the country have made efforts to strengthen laws on criminal procedure and to demand new ones.

Stiff punishment has proved an effective deterrent to crime in many places. As Seymour Gelber, assistant state attorney in Dade County (Miami) Florida, says: "If a judge gives a stiff sentence, the news gets around. A judge in Key West got the reputation—five years for robbery, not six months or a year—and criminals stayed away."

For the protection of *everybody's* rights today, we must treat criminals as criminals, and not as misguided "patients" to be coddled, counseled, and set loose to prey on further victims.

No!

1. *It is misrepresentation of the facts to blame the Supreme Court for the rising crime rate.*

The increase in crime reflects the fact that the people coming out of the post-World War II population boom have reached adolescence—the age group accounting for the highest percentage of criminal behavior in this country. Decisions by the Supreme Court and lower courts dealing with criminal procedure have little or no influence on their actions.

David Acheson, former U. S. Attorney for the District of Columbia, argues the point this way: "Changes in court decisions and prosecution procedure have about the same effect on crime rates as would have an aspirin on a brain tumor." U. S. Deputy Attorney General Ramsey Clark agrees. "Court rules," he explains, "do not cause crimes. People do not commit crimes . . . because they feel they will *not* be convicted. We as a people commit crimes because we are capable of committing crimes. We *choose* to commit crimes."

The courts are concrete pillars of law and order, not wobbly bamboo poles. Our country has a larger percentage of its population in prison than any other Western country. According to the U. S. Department of Justice, from seventy to eighty per cent of all persons indicted throughout the U. S. are convicted. And they usually receive stiff sentences. Each year U. S. judges hand down some 15,000 sentences of five years (or more) in prison.

2. *The Supreme Court has a duty to protect the rights of all citizens —including those accused of crime.*

The first eight Amendments to the Constitution were specifically designed to limit police power and to protect citizens from government oppression. For generations local police may have gotten away with ignoring some of these Constitutional protections in criminal cases. Now they're complaining because they are being forced to observe them. As Yale Kamisar, a professor at the University of Michigan Law School, asks: "When, if ever, weren't law enforcement personnel impatient with the checks and balances of our system? When, if ever, didn't they feel limited? When, if ever, will they realize that our citizens are free *because* the police are *limited?*"

The Supreme Court rulings will particularly protect the innocent person who is not aware of his Constitutional rights. It is he, not the hardened criminal, who is most likely to be intimidated by illegal police "pressure" tactics. It is he who needs to be told right away what his Constitutional rights are.

Because of recent Supreme Court decisions, many states are busy modernizing old codes of criminal procedure and devising new techniques to meet present conditions. A more equitable system of criminal justice will result. And the new system, many authorities agree, will encourage better training, higher pay, and greater public support for the police.

The preservation of our Constitutional guarantee and the even-handed administration of justice are worth the chance that a guilty man will occasionally escape punishment.

3. *The U. S. can still attack crime effectively without stepping on anyone's rights.*

Psychologists, social workers, and criminologists have made great strides in the past 60 years in understanding the criminal mind. With new tools they have discovered numerous factors involved in criminal behavior. By introducing modern concepts—rehabilitation, psychiatric help, counseling, and retraining—they have taken minor steps toward limiting the recurrence of crime.

Centuries of hangings and floggings failed to eliminate or even decrease crime. "Stiffer and stiffer punishments never helped anybody," says Professor Howard F. Gill, an expert on penal administration at American University. And where authorities have attempted to toughen up their approach to crime, they have met with failure.

The problems to be solved are difficult. Failures will still occur. But reverting to a medieval bread-and-water approach to justice would be foolish.

What Do You Think?

Which argument seems the stronger? Why?

2.   ARE OUR PRISONS EFFECTIVE?

Prisons—are they effective? What does "effective" mean? Do they help to prevent crime? Is their role one of punishment or rehabilitation? The two readings which follow discuss what prisons are, and what they should be.

Who Goes to Prison? *

Most of the people who commit crimes which could send them to prison do not go, argues the author. Prison populations reflect only that part of the criminal world that isn't smart, rich, dishonest, or lucky enough to stay out of jail. What do you think?

---

* Excerpted from Bruce Jackson, "Who Goes to Prison: Caste and Careerism in Crime," *The Atlantic Monthly,* January 1965. Copyright © 1965 by the Atlantic Monthly Company, Boston, Mass. 02116. Reprinted with permission.

The men who become prisoners are the most obvious criminals: clumsy, stupid, impulsive, hungup. Some have gotten what they deserve, some are oversentenced, some belong in mental institutions, some shouldn't be in any institution.

Most of the people who commit crimes which could send them to prison do not go. Consider, for example, the large number of criminals who go unpunished simply because the general public insists on cooperating with them. Call girls, bookies, loan sharks, abortionists, and bootleggers know quite well that their customers are as anxious to keep their activities from the attention of the police as they are themselves, that even if an arrest does occur, most honest citizens will do whatever they can to avoid involvement. . . .

Other crimes go unreported, and there is no way to document their number. No one knows how many public officials take graft in any single year, but surely there are many more than those who make the headlines. Many business firms will not prosecute shoplifters, embezzlers, or pilferers, because they believe the damage to their reputation will be more costly than the satisfaction that might result from a conviction. Many rapes, for exactly the same reason, go unreported: victims think there will be no apprehension or conviction of the criminal and they will suffer embarrassment in addition to their humiliation (not without some cause: there were convictions of adults on the original charge in only 16.7 per cent of the rapes reported to the police in 1963).

*   *   *   *   *

The deliberate and intelligent offenders—the professional killer, the high-level narcotics distributor, the fraudulent corporation executive, the thoughtful burglar, the physician salting away money which ought to be paid to the IRS—go to prison so rarely they hardly affect the statistics. And when they do go, they do not stay very long. Prison population reflects only that part of the criminal world that isn't smart, rich, dishonest, or lucky enough to stay out of jail. . . .

Since the professionals are the most articulate and agile members of the criminal population, it is not surprising to find that on the rare occasions when they have to do some time, they rise quickly to positions of power in the prison society. Even though they are few in number, their influence is often extensive. In Texas, the professional is called a "character," and one of them explained at some length just what the qualifications were and how one's status in the world outside affected one's inmate career:

"Crimewise you have a differentiation. First of all, you've got your rapos and you've got your women beaters and your women killers and your incests and all of these crimes against another person that is more or less unprotected. Now those people are looked way down on. Because we know that they will do it to my wife or your wife or our children just like they'll do it to anybody else.

"Your real characters are ones that go out and use the underworld as a means of livelihood and go about it in a professional way, in a professional manner. . . . I think that a character is somebody that makes his living completely outside the law but yet has some principle about it. And you'd be surprised at the difference in the way the police treat us."

*   *   *   *   *

Even if it were not true that the poor and stupid are shortchanged in the police station and courthouse, they surely are after they get to prison. Parole boards are generally composed of reasonable, honest, well-meaning men, and when an inmate comes before them, they consider with as much fairness as they can muster his past record, his conduct while in prison, the likelihood of his success outside. What determines the likelihood of success? The man's economic situation, his associates, his place of habitation. The offender with money or connections can easily demonstrate that he will be able to get along without difficulty; so can most professional criminals. The noncriminal impulse offender and the professional tend to serve time quietly in prison; they're smart enough to stay out of trouble. But the offender whose social and intellectual inadequacies were responsible for his getting into trouble in the first place—where will he go and what will he do?

The answers are obvious: back to the same street, the old crowd, the old routine. It is not surprising that he doesn't find early release. No wonder that he spends a long time behind bars. No wonder, but no fairer. We can understand why the poor go to jail more frequently than the affluent, why the smart spend less time behind bars than the stupid, but we should understand also that this same set of conditions makes the failures more antisocial, more bitter.

David Haughey commented on the effect of this: "From the inside, this certainly is part of what leads the average inmate to feel that he is the victim of a corrupt society, and that everyone on the outside is just as corrupt as he is. It's just that they have more things going for them—friends, money, influence, power. And when you don't have power, then you serve time."

That inside view is, unfortunately, the correct one.

What Do You Think?

1.   What picture does the author present of the average individual sent to prison? What evidence does he offer in support of

his statement that "most of the people who commit crimes which could send them to prison do not go"?

2. Is Jackson's article likely to be endorsed by those who advocate increasing the length of prison sentences as a means of reducing crime? Why or why not?

"I Lost My Number and Got Back My Name" *

Here is a description of a somewhat unusual type of prison in Chino, California. The author, appointed Superintendent of the California Institution for Men at Chino in 1940, describes a different pattern for the care and treatment of men in trouble. What is the reasoning behind his actions?

America cannot solve her crime problem by locking men in prison. Neither can she adjust men in prison and prepare them for the day of release by dumping them into a great bastille.

It is a well-recognized fact today that a prison experience is apt to bring out the worst in a man and leave its permanent scar upon his personality. Therefore what happens to men in prison will in large measure determine their attitude upon release. Now ninety-eight per cent of those who go to prison return to the community some day. We should be greatly concerned whether they come out soured and embittered against society for having placed them there or full of hope and new courage for the future because we have afforded them ample opportunity to improve their condition during incarceration.

One reason for clinging to outmoded prison traditions of the past is the fundamental fear that men will escape if given the slightest opportunity. So we continue to build our prisons of concrete and steel, with clanging doors and electric locks, with armed guards and barbed wire, on the old theory that since we cannot determine who can be trusted and who cannot, we must treat all men alike, expecting them all to escape.

I am certain that the sternest warden of our penal institutions in America will admit that if he had the proper facilities in the form of different types of institutions for different types of prisoners, and the necessary trained personnel to sort out and place the hardened and dangerous offenders in the proper maximum-security institution, he would need such a secure unit for not more than twenty-five per cent of all his prisoners. The rest could be handled in medium- and minimum-security institutions. . . .

And yet with few exceptions our states have been unwilling to support

---

* Excerpted from Kenyon J. Scudder, "The Open Institution," *Annals of the American Academy of Political and Social Science,* CCXCIII, May, 1954.

any change in their penal systems, content to go on as before. The majority of the prisons of the world are still of a maximum-security type, surrounded by high walls bristling with guns and other restrictive devices. . . .

THE CALIFORNIA STORY

Under the leadership of Richard A. McGee, director of corrections, and with the splendid backing of former Governor Earl Warren, the prison system of California has been completely overhauled; new medium- and minimum-security prisons and a new institution for women have been built, two reception-guidance centers have been set up, in the north and south, and a medical facility for those in need of such service, thus providing a statewide system of classification and treatment of all offenders regardless of the seriousness of their crime.

The real beginning of these changes . . . occurred in 1935 when an enlightened legislature decided that prisoners should be treated as individuals and that the more helpful cases should be separated from the hardened offenders. To that end provision was made for the "segregation" from the hardened criminals of those prisoners capable of moral rehabilitation and restoration to good citizenship.

A farm-type institution with suitable buildings and program was proposed, and a site of 2,600 acres was secured near the town of Chino in southern California. . . .

OPPORTUNITY KNOCKS

In 1940, I was appointed superintendent at Chino and given a free hand to select my staff. Here was such an opportunity as seldom comes to a state more than once in a century, to start a new type of institution for the first offender. The brutal and impersonal treatment I had witnessed at the hands of ignorant and untrained guards in institutions where I had worked convinced me that there should be some better method of dealing with prisoners if they were to be restored to useful citizenship. Why not weave into this new fabric the best we could find in the good prisons in America and develop a different pattern for the care and treatment of men in trouble?

Here, emphasis would be placed on freedom of choice, acceptance of responsibility while in prison, and preparation for return to community life. We would recognize that individuals change slowly; therefore, the process of adjustment must be gradual. It is easy to be good with a gun in your back when you are told what to do and when to do it. It is quite another thing to have to accept responsibility while in prison, the kind of responsibility you are expected to assume in a free world outside the walls. We must follow a new prison philosophy, namely, "that there can be no regeneration except in freedom. That rehabilitation must come from within the individual and not through coercion."

CHINO'S STAFF

In selecting our staff, why not look for young men just out of college, who perhaps had never seen a prison; young men with vision and courage and a desire for a career in penology? Then we should not be tied down by old traditions binding us to the many outmoded methods of the past. And since we were not going to build the inside wall with its five additional gun towers, we should be forced to rely upon the personality, ability, and courage of the staff to handle the men without the use of force and firearms. . . .

These young men were given an intensive eight weeks' training course before we were ready to open the prison. The course included instruction in the use of firearms so that no one would get hurt. Then we locked up the guns, and they have never been used except in case of escapes. Through the teaching of judo, the art of self-defense, we developed in each man poise, courage, and confidence in his own ability to deal with any emergency that might arise without resorting to arms. A part of each day was devoted to the theory of handling men, some sociology, psychology, problems of discipline, and the general philosophy of freedom that was to govern the institution.

THE FIRST BUS LOAD OF PRISONERS

We had quite a discussion about how to transport our first load of men from San Quentin to Chino. Old-timers said we should get a prison car with locks and bars, handcuffs, and leg irons or we would never get them there.

We had personally interviewed each man, and he had been carefully selected to make the trip. Many had families in southern California, mothers, wives, and children whom they had not seen in months or years, lasting ties that should anchor the men to Chino. Eagerly they inquired about the visiting privileges, whether the family or friends could come to see them.

"My wife can make it up here to San Quentin only once a year," one man said, "and then she can't bring the baby."

"Do you really think I can make it?" another inquired. "I'd like to write my wife."

"Go ahead and write her," I said, "for you will be one of the men to open the institution at Chino."

On July 10, 1941, instead of a prison car we chartered a Greyhound bus and took the first group the five hundred miles to Chino as ordinary passengers. There were thirty-four convicts and three of us. We had no handcuffs, leg irons, billy clubs, or guns, and there was no lock on the bus door.

We arrived at Chino at six o'clock that night. I couldn't have asked for a better-behaved group.

As the young, unarmed supervisor, dressed in sport clothes, waved us through the front gate, a new institution was born, based upon this new philosophy of freedom.

The reaction of the men was something to remember. That night we waded through the mail home: "Dear Mom: You don't have to be ashamed of getting letters out of this place because it isn't a prison. It's the California Institution for Men." Another said: "Dad: When I arrived, I lost my number and got back my name 'cause they call me Jack around here."

ESCAPES

At Chino, we endeavor to take all the glory from escaping. "There are certain responsibilities you must carry," [prisoners] are told.

"First, you must decide whether you are going to stay here or escape. It's easy to get out of here. Let us tell you how to get over the fence. Just take your jacket, throw it over the barbed wire and over you go— and you won't cut yourself getting out. If you stay on the inside of the fence you can enjoy limited freedom. When you drop down on the other side you are a fugitive felon and we will bring you back no matter how long it takes. Many more years will be added to your sentence and you can never come back to Chino."

Fear of escapes dominates every institution. It magnifies itself and becomes a challenge, especially in the absence of a proper classification system and institutional facilities to serve the different types of prisoners. When these are present, escapes are few.

The offense a man committed has little to do with his selection for Chino. We have everything from murder to passing bad checks. The selection is based on the man himself, on his attitude, and whether he is likely to get into trouble again. . . .

DISCIPLINE

Discipline in a minimum-security prison must be handled on a fair and impartial basis. How can we maintain order when fear is removed?

Men in prison, with the exception of the 25 per cent who must be confined in maximum security, do not want trouble. They want to get out and to do it in the right way, and they will respond to just treatment.

By means of a disciplinary committee, all cases involving serious infractions are given a fair and thorough hearing. If the man cannot get along with other people or has refused to cooperate with the institution officials and program, he is removed from the group until he is willing to do so. We have no isolation unit at Chino. No man is sent to segregation for any stated length of time. . . . We have no restricted diet, every man getting the same food as others, even to his dessert, although he may be locked up and not allowed to go to the dining room.

A man is placed in segregation only until he declares that he can behave himself and is now able to get along with other people. . . .

VISITING PRIVILEGES

In a minimum-security prison, liberal visiting privileges help to develop further an atmosphere of freedom and to place responsibility upon the individual inmate. . . .

Statistics showed that men on parole had a much better chance to succeed where the family had been kept together. In order to encourage family visiting, the men were allowed to build a beautiful visiting area outside the Administration Building. They constructed a large pergola, planted lawn and trees, and built many varicolored picnic tables. Here the family unit could visit together on Saturdays, Sundays, and holidays.

When you visit at Chino, you can bring the children and a picnic lunch. Over the loudspeaker a voice calls,

"Will Mr. Johnson come in and meet his guest."

As Mr. Johnson appears, his little girl runs across the room and jumps into her daddy's arms; while he holds her closely, the wife comes up with the food basket. He embraces his wife and picks up the basket.

"Come on out to the visiting grounds."

The wife looks around and says, "But where are the guards?"

"There are no guards here, honey," he replies. "Come on. I'm the host." And for four hours the little family can visit undisturbed with no one listening in to the conversation.

The men say, "It's a wonderful thing to be able to visit with your children and not have them forget you while you're in prison." . . .

WORK, WORK TRAINING, RECREATION

The Department of Corrections has emphasized the importance of constructive useful work, and in our prison industries or in the many other tasks to be performed all men work seven and a half hours a day. . . .

Classes in bricklaying, tile setting, plastering, welding, machine shop work, body and fender repair, auto mechanics, and a host of others, taught by journeymen instructors furnished by the Chino High School District, furnish men with skills to sell to an employer upon release.

This is of great importance in a prisoner's ultimate adjustment, because our records indicate that 85 per cent of the men who go to prison have no special skills to make them employable. . . .

Men in prison must be kept busy in useful work and wholesome recreation for their leisure hours. The recreation program ranges from football to checkers. Music, radio, television, dramatics, play their important part. . . .

RELIGION

There is an important place for religion and spiritual counseling in every prison in the world. Too often it is overlooked or pushed aside, the last thing for which adequate provision is made. It calls for carefully selected and well-trained chaplains who have a genuine interest in the welfare of prisoners. When the religious program is sincere, the men will respond. . . .

SOCIAL LIVING

Men in prison often fear the day of release. How will society receive them? Will there be a whispering campaign against them in the neighborhood? What about traffic, bright lights, noise and confusion in public places? Will they be able to meet and converse with people?

One night . . . the California Community Players from Pasadena played *Charlie's Aunt* for our men. There were twenty-two in the cast. About forty of our men helped to put on the show. Afterwards Mrs. Scudder invited the cast over to the house for refreshments, and with them the forty men. It was raining outside when they arrived.

There were about seventy people in our living room. Things were a little tense at first. Then Mrs. Scudder opened the door to her dining room and we all went in for refreshments. The table with its lace cloth, candles, silver service, and flowers was a beautiful sight. We each picked up our ice cream, cake, and coffee and went back to the living room. Some sat on the floor, others stood in front of the fire. Then with the food came a hum of conversation. One of the men went to the piano and began to play the songs America loves to sing, "Home on the Range," "Let Me Call You Sweetheart," and the whole house burst into song. . . .

They were all people together, but forty of them were reaching out for the precious thing called freedom and trying to get it back again, for now they realized what they had lost.

CLASSIFICATION AND SELECTION

In setting up a minimum-security institution in any state adequate facilities must be provided for the proper classification and selection of men from the prison system. A few wrong selections can cause a lot of trouble.

One of the best means of selection is the facility known as a reception-guidance center. In California, instead of prisoners being sent by the courts to any particular prison they are committed to the State Department of Corrections, and the director instructs the sheriffs of the various counties to deliver them to the guidance centers. . . . At these centers an able staff of trained psychologists, psychiatrists, social workers, and counselors study them for a period of two months before any final action is taken on which prison they shall be sent to. . . .

PAROLE

Available figures indicate that the rate of failure on parole is much lower from Chino than from the other institutions in the state. We should expect that, because these men are carefully selected as the better prospects for successful adjustment if kept away from the hardened offender.

RECENT PROGRESS

In the past twenty-five years several states have made real progress in the care and treatment of men in prison. They have abolished the silence system and the striped clothing; mail and visiting privileges have been improved; and men are being classified and trained for useful work. These few privileges were granted over the years in spite of a hue and cry that prisoners were being coddled and that trouble would surely follow. But trouble did not follow. Instead, in these few prisons men are being better prepared for the day of release.

WHAT OF THE FUTURE?

And what does all this treatment of adults in prison add up to?

Simply this. If we can successfully adjust men in prison after they have run the whole gamut of the law, if we can get them over the fear of work, if we can send them back to society a little better than when they entered, then how much more sensible it would be if we could reach these cases earlier in life before the damage has been done. Reach them in the early years of childhood before they become delinquent, before we allow them to enter upon a criminal career. We make our criminals in this country. They are not born into crime. Then why not place our emphasis upon prevention by reaching these cases at the source of trouble —in the average community?

What Do You Think?

1. How would you react to Scudder's statement that "what happens to men in prison will in large measure determine their attitude upon release." Explain.
2. Would you support Scudder's approach to the treatment of prisoners? Why or why not?

3. WHAT ABOUT THE DEATH PENALTY?

Capital punishment (more commonly referred to as the "death penalty") has in recent years stirred a storm of worldwide controversy.

In the two articles that follow, you will be presented with an argument for and against this practice. Which seems the strongest?

A Police Chief's Views on Capital Punishment *

The following have frequently been offered as arguments against capital punishment:

1. Capital punishment does not deter crime.
2. It "brutalizes" human nature.
3. The rich and powerful often escape the death penalty.
4. Swift and certain punishment is more effective.
5. Society is to blame for the criminal's way of life, so we ought to be more considerate of him.

Let us, then, apart from the demands of pure justice, which should be the only determining factor, examine the above claims for validity and provability.

CAPITAL PUNISHMENT DOES NOT DETER CRIME?

If this be true, then why do criminals fear it most? Why does every criminal sentenced to death seek commutation to life imprisonment? Common sense alone, without the benefit of knowledge, wisdom, and experience, convinces that we are influenced to the greatest degree by that which we love, respect, or fear to the greatest degree—and that we cling most tenaciously to our most valued possessions. Life is indisputably our greatest possession. Additionally, there is no definitive proof anywhere that the death penalty is not a deterrent. There are merely the gratuitous statements of wishful thinkers, some of whom, because of the responsible duties of their positions, ought not be making unprovable or misleading statements.

It is also put forth, by those who would weaken our laws . . . that many murderers on death row claim they did not think of the death penalty when they committed their crimes. This is undoubtedly true. That is precisely the point. If they had thought of it, they would not have committed their crimes. . . . What of the countless others who *were* deterred from murder through fear of the penalty? . . .

IT BRUTALIZES HUMAN NATURE?

But the opposite is true. Wanton *murder* brutalizes human nature and cheapens human life, not the penalty for its perpetration. Capital punishment is the guarantee against murder and the brutalization of human nature. . . . To allow heinous criminals to commit their crimes

---

* Excerpted from Edward J. Allen, "Capital Punishment: Your Protection and Mine," *The Police Chief*, XXVII, June, 1960.

without the commensurate reparation of the death penalty would surely brutalize and degrade human nature and reduce society to a state of barbarism.

THE RICH AND POWERFUL GENERALLY ESCAPE?

There is truth in this statement and it is equally applicable to other penalties. . . . No one decries this discrimination more than law enforcement. . . . Since justice does not *always* prevail, ought we abandon our striving for its attainment? Who would advocate the abolition of the Ten Commandments because they are honored more in their breach than in their observance? . . .

SPECIOUS ARGUMENTS

Two of the reasons advanced for the abolition of the death penalty have no validity whatsoever. One is an attempt to equate human slavery with capital punishment. The argument is this: Slavery was once rampant, but now an enlightened society favors its abolition; therefore, we ought to do away with capital punishment, since we "moderns" are more "enlightened" than our forebears.

Firstly, slavery never was . . . morally right or justifiable or just. The death penalty *is* morally right and justifiable and just. . . . Here is another "beaut" from a university psychiatrist: The death penalty could be society's way of "projecting its own crime into the criminal." Now, I submit that the longer we permit this type of nonsense to be spread abroad, the more ridiculous our nation is going to appear in the eyes of the world. . . .

It is obvious to anyone who believes in the moral and natural law . . . that first-degree murder requires personal premeditation and the full consent of the will, hence, its punishment should be meted out to the criminal or criminals personally responsible. To argue otherwise is to argue the unnatural, but admittedly, this is the day of the unnatural logician.

SWIFT AND CERTAIN PUNISHMENT

Swift and certain punishment is assuredly a crime deterrent, but only when coupled with commensurate severity. . . .

INDIVIDUAL STATES AND CAPITAL PUNISHMENT

The proponents for abolition make much of the fact that there were seven states in 1958 . . . which have abolished capital punishment. These proponents make no mention of the fact that eight other states . . . once abolished capital punishment and have returned to it. . . .

The highest murder rate . . . was the southern group of 13 states. They had the exceptionally high rate of 9.0. Admittedly, the South has a problem, but the removal of the death penalty would only aggravate it. . . .

It would appear that the permeance of racial, ethnic, and religio-political cultures influence crime rates, including murder, in the various geographical sections of our country. Common sense dictates that more severe punitive sanctions are necessary in those states or sections where serious crime is more prevalent. . . . It would be the height of folly therefore to advocate the removal of the death penalty throughout the Southern States where the crime of murder is a serious threat.

Where crime and murder are at a low level and where community life is governed by respect and reverence for law, rather than by its enforcement, then severe punitive measures may be relaxed, but not abolished. . . .

CONCLUSION

Of course, the overwhelming statistic . . . is that forty-one of the fifty states and the majority of the nations in the world have the death penalty. . . .

All of the erudition, wisdom, experience, and knowledge of history reveals that the death penalty is morally and legally just. For the just man or nation this should be sufficient. Even so, justice is still justice, if no man is just—were it not so, God would have told us.

Statement on Capital Punishment *

Governor Edmund G. Brown
January 31, 1963
To the Senate and Assembly of the Legislature of California:
I ask this Legislature to enact a moratorium on capital punishment.
It is my personal conviction we should abolish the death penalty entirely.

I.

The trend among humane and forward-looking state and national governments is toward diminution of the death penalty. Even jurisdictions which refuse to abolish it have become increasingly selective in its application. In the three decades since 1930, the national average of state executions has shrunk from 167 to 72 a year.

You know where I stand. I oppose capital punishment because it weakens the very society it is meant to protect; because it shames the public conscience and denies the entire rehabilitative concept of modern penology.

---

* Statement of Governor Edmund G. Brown on Capital Punishment. Submitted to the Legislature of the State of California, Thursday, January 31, 1963.

I oppose capital punishment because it is more vengeful than punitive; because it is more an act of hate than of justice. We kill the murderer because we fear him, not because he is beyond rehabilitation or
control. We kill him not for his crime but in the blind hope that others
may not commit his crime.

And we can take no pride from the knowledge that we often equate
the darkness of a man's crime with the darkness of his skin—his right
to live with the rightness of his status in life.

I oppose capital punishment, too, because it brutalizes man; because
a society that takes human life cannot invest its citizens with respect for
human life.

To those who invoke the ancient code, "an eye for an eye, a tooth
for a tooth," I answer that society must live by an ethic and an intelligence above that of the homicidal psychotic. The murderer most often
kills in the heat of passion and with only a moment's forethought. But
we who judge him kill coolly and with long premeditation.

Let us invoke, rather, the Biblical commandment, "Thou shalt not
kill," and apply it as rigidly to the state as we now apply it to citizens
of the state.

I recognize there is no clear consensus among us on the moral justice or injustice of capital punishment. Nor is there consensus on the
compassion we should or should not feel for those who have died, and
who now await death, at our hands.

For that reason, I will not center my present argument for a moratorium on the controversial grounds of public morality or pity for the
lowest members of an imperfect society. Rather, I will confine my case
in chief to that which is not debatable in the light of reason and of historical knowledge:

The failure of capital punishment to deter capital crime.

*The unjust and unpredictable enforcement of the death penalty in
California.*

II.

Punishment is a deterrent to crime only if it is swift and certain.
But of all major crimes, the punishment for homicide is most subject to
the law's delay and to the inconsistencies of our courts.

The evidence is clear. In 1961 there were 609 homicides in California. Only 106 defendants were found guilty of first degree murder
and only 20 were given the sentence of death.

How can it be argued that our gas chamber is an effective deterrent
if only one murderer in 30 is actually sent to Death Row?

Of the 20 who did receive death sentences for murder in 1961, only
five went to the gas chamber by January 1, 1963. Of the remaining 15,

one already has won a reversal of penalty and three more will win reversals if the historical ratio pertains. As Governor, I have given executive clemency to another four, commuting their sentences to life without possibility of parole.

It is probable, then, that only 12 of the 609 murderers actually will surrender their lives to the state. What possible deterrence can there be in a penalty we invoke only 2 per cent of the time?

My argument would not stand if we put to death all murderers who were found to be sane. Then, at least, punishment would be certain, if not swift. But I cannot believe a person contemplating murder is much afraid of a penalty he has 49 chances in 50 of escaping.

I will concede our random enforcement of the death penalty in California is not in itself an all-convincing argument against deterrence.

The incontrovertible proof is to be found in those states and nations which have given up the death penalty. In no instance has there been a meaningful increase in homicides after abolition. To the contrary, many states and nations without capital punishment have an incidence of murder below that of contiguous and comparable jurisdictions where the death penalty is in effect.

States without the death penalty, or with minimum enforcement of it rank among the lowest in homicides. Yet 12 southern states, all of whom enforce the death penalty vigorously, have the highest incidence of murder.

If capital punishment is not a deterrent, what arguments are left to its defenders?

Retribution—society's right to avenge itself against the offender?

Society has no such right. The purpose of punishment is to rehabilitate or control, not destroy.

Self-protection—the certainty that a dead murderer can never repeat his crime?

Recidivism is rare among first degree murderers who are given parole. The bandit or kidnaper is far more likely to commit murder after his release—and the record proves it. Should we, then, execute all who have been found guilty of crimes of violence?

Capital punishment not only fails to deter capital crime but is actually an obstruction to the swift and certain administration of justice.

The reluctance of many juries to impose it often permits the first degree murderer to escape with a second degree or manslaughter conviction.

The division of murder cases into three separate trials for guilt, sanity, and penalty is costly to the taxpayer and wasteful of the time and resources of a court system whose calendar is already oppressive.

We confine the issue of sanity almost entirely to murder cases, requiring the services of psychiatrists for both defense and prosecution and giving rise to the persistent controversy over the modern application of the M'Naghten Rules.

Only last week a man went to his death in our gas chamber who was found to be mentally sick but legally sane. The sophistry of such distinctions should torture the conscience of us all.

And let us admit the law is subject to error—the ugly chance we might condemn the innocent.

III.

Our hit or miss enforcement of the death penalty in California is not unlike a wheel of chance.

We execute the man but let the woman live for identical crimes.

Indeed, the odds against the murderer change with the weapon he chooses. If he shoots his victim, the odds favor his execution. If he bludgeons or poisons his victim, the odds favor life imprisonment.

Even in advance of his trial he gambles with his life. Should he plead guilty and hope for leniency from the court? Or should he plead not guilty and risk death?

There are in Death Row today felons awaiting execution for crimes identical in degree and extenuation to those for which other prisoners are serving life terms with possibility of parole.

The murderer even gambles on the jurisdiction in which he commits his crime. There are counties in California in which juries have never sent a murderer to Death Row.

Is it just that such abstract elements should decide the issue of life or death? I think not.

We come now to one of the most damning indictments of the death penalty. It is a fact that we sentence to death members of minority races, the poor, the unintelligent, and the friendless for crimes we are prone to minimize in defendants who are more like ourselves.

The Negro who kills in a robbery is much more likely to die in our gas chamber than the influential executive who kills for community property.

Can we deny that capital punishment imposes a further, and fatal discrimination against those among us who already are the most common victims of bigotry and prejudice?

As for the poor of all races, it is clear we execute them in disproportionate numbers because they lack the resources to retain the most skillful counsel or to press their cases to the ultimate.

I submit to you, then, that a moratorium not only would support the case against deterrence but would banish the inequities that plague our present enforcement of the death penalty. And we must banish them as an act of public conscience.

Can we not join those states and nations which recognize that no society is infallible in its judgments and that no man is beyond hope— beyond our power and God's to redeem him?

> Respectfully submitted,
> Edmund G. Brown
> Governor

January 31, 1963

What Do You Think?

1. Summarize Chief Allen's views on capital punishment. What evidence does he offer in support of his views?

2. Allen argues that "all of the erudition, wisdom, experience, and knowledge of history reveals that the death penalty is morally and legally just." What evidence might a student of history present to support or refute his argument?

3. Summarize Governor Brown's argument toward capital punishment. What evidence does he offer to support his case?

4. What, if any, do you think is Brown's most telling point? Explain.

5. Who do you think has the strongest case—Brown or Allen? Explain.

4. GUN CONTROLS: INDISPENSABLE OR IRRESPONSIBLE? *

In the past, the control of firearms in the United States has been left to the states and cities, with the consequence that existing laws vary widely. Many people argued that federal legislation was necessary. The assassinations of Martin Luther King, Jr. and Senator Robert Kennedy brought a sense of urgency to the issue.

In 1968, Congress passed a bill that:

1. banned the interstate mail order sale of rifles, shotguns, and ammunition (a similar provision about handguns was passed earlier that year);

2. put restrictions on over-the-counter sales of firearms to persons who are not residents of the state where the gun is purchased;

3. banned the sale of rifles and shotguns to persons under 18 years of age and handguns to persons under 21.

Many felt that the bill was too weak. Are stronger gun laws indispensable to the preservation of law and order in our society? Here are arguments on opposing sides of the issue.

---

* "Gun Controls: Indispensable or Irresponsible?" *Senior Scholastic,* December 7, 1967. By permission *Senior Scholastic.* © 1967 Scholastic Magazines, Inc.

Indispensable!

1. *Stronger gun controls would save thousands of lives each year.*

In the time it takes to read this article, someone in the U. S. will die as a result of an incident involving firearms. In fact, every day in the U. S. approximately 50 people die from firearms—through murder, accidents, and suicide.

Even more significant, says author-critic Carl Bakal, is the fact that since the turn of the century this "plague" has brought death to the astounding total of more than 750,000 Americans—men, women, and children. This is more than all of our nation's war deaths combined, from the Revolution to Viet Nam.

Something must be done to halt this slaughter, which partially results from the easy accessibility of firearms. [Said] Sen. Robert F. Kennedy (D., N. Y.): "If we do not pass these laws, we sign the death warrant of more policemen and more children who will be caught in tomorrow's crossfire. If we act now, we can save hundreds of lives in this country and spare thousands of families . . . the grief and heartbreak that may come from the loss of a husband, a son, a brother, or a friend."

The enactment of effective federal legislation to keep firearms out of the wrong hands has been repeatedly blocked by special interest groups who are more interested in selling guns than in safety. After all, no one is asking that the sale of guns be banned—only controlled to keep weapons away from the unstable and criminal elements in society. The *Washington Post* put it this way in an editorial: "It (federal gun control) would save the lives of a great number of decent citizens who, when you come to think about it, are entitled to a little consideration, too."

2. *Present gun-control laws are ineffective.*

It's true that some states now have strong gun control laws. But what about states that don't? New Jersey law, for example, requires a would be purchaser of arms and/or ammunition to submit to fingerprinting, a criminal records check, and (if it's deemed necessary) a psychiatric examination. But no one in New Jersey really has to bother with all that red tape to get a gun. It's easier to drive across the border into New York or Pennsylvania to make the purchase. Shortly after passage of the New Jersey gun law, dealers in parts of New York and Pennsylvania—which border on New Jersey—reported sales up as much as ninety per cent!

Today's federal laws may do some good in keeping machine guns out of the hands of deranged persons and would-be killers, but what good does that do when anyone can easily obtain pistols and rifles? Let's face it, current federal laws mainly regulate the sale of weapons normally used only by hardened criminals anyway. What is needed is a law aimed at keeping all types of guns out of the hands of potentially dangerous persons.

No one claims that any law can be foolproof. A seemingly normal person—who under any circumstances would be permitted to own a gun—can go berserk and go on a killing rampage. But stricter laws at least would help keep guns out of the hands of those persons *known* to be dangerous, such as the emotionally disturbed and known criminals. And only the federal government has the power to make such laws meaningful and enforceable.

As former U. S. Attorney General Nicholas de B. Katzenbach put it: "Which is more significant, the right not to be slightly inconvenienced in the purchase of a firearm, or the right not to be terrorized, robbed, wounded, or killed?"

3. *Federal gun controls would not violate the Constitution.*

For many years those who would block further gun control by the federal government have turned to the words of the Second Amendment to the U. S. Constitution, claiming it guarantees citizens a Constitutional right to bear arms.

But contrary to what they say—and what many others accept without question—the Second Amendment does *not* guarantee the *individual* the right to bear arms. The Amendment clearly connects the right to bear arms with the needs of a state militia. This clause was written when the security of the states, following the Revolution, was still a matter of uneasy concern. But state militias play a relatively minor role in U. S. security today.

Responding to the argument that requiring a license for guns would violate the rights of individuals, U. S. Representative James H. Scheuer (D., N. Y.), a member of the National Rifle Association (NRA) and winner of four of its National Championship medals, said: "It's insanity to believe that my civil rights are being violated by having to have a pistol permit. No responsible citizen can in good conscience deny the urgent need to protect the public from arming the destructive, deranged, dangerous, and irresponsible persons among us."

Irresponsible!

1. *Further gun controls would violate a basic Constitutional guarantee.*

The Second Amendment to the U. S. Constitution states: "The right of the people to keep and bear arms shall not be infringed." This is a right the citizens of this nation have had since its founding. It is a right that recognizes that a man can defend his home against all intruders. And it's therefore *not* out of date.

Rather than taking away rights, the government should encourage citizens to learn more about weapons so they could use them effectively and wisely if ever called upon in an emergency. Look what happened this summer when the National Guard was called in to help quell riots. Some soldiers in these units were so poorly trained and inexperienced that several were accused of shooting bystanders. Others, with itchy trigger fingers, accidentally fired on their own men. But you can't expect to have a well-trained militia if men are allowed to handle weapons only at once-a-week meetings.

An even more significant aspect of the Constitutional right to bear arms is that it shows—not just to us, but to the entire world—that the U. S. is a free country. When all citizens have the right to bear arms a country is indeed free. No dictatorship could afford such confidence, and none does. When people have the freedom to bear arms it is they who hold the power of the state rather than any single arbitrary force.

As Benjamin Franklin once said: "Those who would give up essential liberty to purchase a little temporary safety deserve neither liberty nor safety."

2. *Gun controls would help criminals more than protect law-abiding citizens.*

Some weapons invariably fall into the hands of deranged people. But there are nearly 25 million responsible Americans who possess firearms. In fact, it may well be that because they own these weapons they act as a deterrent to crime by others—and thus help to maintain law and order.

Says Mrs. Maria Monplaisir, a leader of New York's Conservative party, in explaining the party's opposition to proposed gun control legislation: "These proposed laws will not reduce crime because they are not really aimed at the criminal who uses a gun in committing a crime, but at the sportsman or hunter who uses a gun for hunting and harmless target shooting."

Nor would gun restrictions stop a determined killer or suicide from achieving his goal. After all, it isn't necessary to use a *gun* to kill a person.

Even where there *are* strict gun laws, murder rates are high. For example, Texas law prohibits the carrying of a handgun either openly or concealed. Yet Dallas, Texas, has the tenth highest murder rate among the country's major cities.

Even more frightening is that gun control laws actually would help the criminal. Says U. S. Representative John D. Dingell (D., Mich.): "Most latter-day legislation aimed at restricting firearms sale, distribution, and usage has the effect of unilaterally disarming the law-abiding. . . . Indeed, I would go so far as to say that it insures the criminal that his proposed victim will be unarmed while he has the advantage both of stealth, choice of time and place for the attack, and also the privilege of having a weapon which would be denied to the law-abiding citizen."

3. *Stricter gun control laws would be difficult to enforce.*

The problem of enforcing stricter gun laws would be staggering—not only in complexity but in cost to the nation's taxpayers. The government itself estimates that in addition to the more than 50 million guns already owned by hunters, collectors, and other sportsmen, "many other millions of firearms—pistols, revolvers, rifles, and shotguns—are owned by citizens determined to protect their families from criminal attack and their property from loss to burglars." That doesn't even take into account the number of guns presently in the hands of criminals. It would be a costly, bureaucratic task even to gather statistics about the guns already in circulation, much less to impose controls on their use.

Moreover, determined criminals can find ways of getting firearms. They could steal them from sportsmen, policemen, and others authorized to have guns, or they could smuggle weapons in from other countries.

Just last month, for example, a gunman walked into a restaurant in Queens, New York, and mowed down three men who, according to police reports, were members of a rival gang. The killer used a machine gun. This proves that despite federal laws criminals are able to get almost any type of gun they want.

As Senator Gordon Allott (R., Colo.) puts it: "There is a problem, but the solution is not to be found in depriving legitimate users of firearms of their liberty to acquire and use them with comparative readiness."

What Do You Think?

Are stricter gun laws indispensable? Explain your reasoning.

5. A COOL LOOK AT THE "CRIME CRISIS" *

Finally, an unusual but perhaps valid view that things are not as bad as they seem. The author, who has been director of the United States Bureau of Prisons since 1937, argues that a "crime crisis" is not really occurring if we look behind the statistics. Is his case a strong one?

Is "serious" crime increasing ominously?

The average newspaper reader's answer to this question is likely

---

* James V. Bennett, "A Cool Look at the Crime Crisis," *Harper's Magazine*, April 1964, by permission of author. Copyright, 1964 Harper's Magazine, Inc.

to be based on highly suspect fare. He reads the crime statistics but he has no way of evaluating them in relation to population, economic conditions, changing laws, and social attitudes. Nor can he judge the relative harmfulness of the many offenses which are recorded. Dramatizing the statistics are the press reports of spectacular crimes, exploits of big-time criminals, and sensational trials.

As a prison director I have a different perspective. For one thing, I think in terms of individuals rather than statistics. I know, of course, that on any given day there are about 220,000 men and women in our state and federal prisons and another 100,000 in local and county jails. Taking the turnover rate into account, we see that approximately a million people spend some time behind bars during the course of a year. But most of them are not the murderers, rapists, and kidnapers pictured by the average citizen.

More than three-fourths of the men and women who are locked up in local jails are drunks, vagrants, mentally ill or defective, or social misfits of other kinds. Of those sentenced to state and federal penitentiaries, more than two-thirds have been convicted of nonviolent crimes such as forgery, auto theft, housebreaking, and larceny. Less than 10 per cent have been found guilty of homicide, rape, or kidnaping.

BEHIND THE STATISTICS

There is a reason to believe that progress is being made in controlling crime if we study the data in depth. For example, in the past thirty-odd years, the homicide rate has been cut nearly in half, dropping from 8.9 per 100,000 of our civilian population in 1930 to 5.1 in 1962.

We have no statistics comparing previous generations with our own. But historians tell us that past ages have been incontestably more lawless. They tell us also that the wholesale application of every cruelty conceivable to the human mind proved futile in reducing crime. The men who ran prisons in medieval and Elizabethan times experimented intensively in the art of administering inhumanity to man—but few experiments in all human history failed so completely.

Among the most disturbing of current statistics are the records of juvenile delinquency—a half-million youngsters are handled by our juvenile courts each year. Certainly, we must take every possible step to redirect them. But we should also use the perspective of time to reassure ourselves that the modern generation is not as black as it is painted. Less than a century ago, as Herbert Asbury pointed out in *The Gangs of New York,* the city swarmed with youngsters who stole, murdered, rioted, and engaged in every form of debauchery. Offsetting today's juvenile delinquency statistics, other figures show that 35 per cent of college-age young people are going to college today in contrast to less than 5 per cent before World War I. The fact is that our young people are doing more to prepare themselves for lives of responsibility than any previous generation.

In evaluating the crime statistics we also ought to ponder the fact that the general prison population of the country is declining. Last year in 27 prison systems the absolute number of inmates declined; in 32 systems the ratio of prisoners to the general population fell.

RACKETEERS AND TEENAGERS

The men and women now in our prisons are individuals with hearts, lungs, and emotions like anyone else. To say this is to invite reproach for "coddling" criminals, a charge frequently made in legislatures and newspaper editorials.

There is a bitter irony in this accusation, for, in fact, the criminal in America is dealt with harshly indeed. Our criminal laws are the most severe in the world, and our legislative bodies are still at work making them more severe. Except possibly for "enemies of the state" in countries where people are sent to prison for political reasons, the American criminal on the average serves several times as long a sentence in prison as his counterpart anywhere else in the world.

The successful defense lawyer knows how to maneuver his case and his client so that they come before an "understanding" judge. But the average defendant is at the mercy of the widely disparate sentences given by different courts in different parts of the country and even by different judges in the same court. A person convicted of homicide in Texas will probably serve about five and a half years, but in Illinois sixteen and a half. For all types of felonies the convicted offender serves about one year in Vermont, but in nearby Rhode Island he averages nearly four. . . .

President Kennedy, whose compassion exceeded that of most men, took an unusual interest in the problems of "equal justice under law" and used his powers of executive clemency to redress judicial savagery. In one case, he cut the life sentence of a teen-age epileptic addict convicted of a narcotics charge (his sentence can be compared with that of Vito Genovese, the alleged kingpin of the American narcotics racket, who got only fifteen years).

To their great credit the federal judges now meet several times a year in seminars and institutes to find ways of minimizing such inequities. But the problem remains.

SHADOWY MINDS

To deplore injustice is not to suggest that we should, in any way, relax our efforts to enforce the law and reduce crime. The dilemma is how best to do it.

The problem is heightened by the fact that a sizable proportion of crimes are committed by psychopaths and mentally sick people. I recall, for example, a bank robber who was known as the Black Phantom. He was an ex-cop who financed affairs with some forty-odd women by holding up banks. After he was caught and committed to a federal prison for observation, we found that he also had a rich fantasy life. He liked to don a black cloak and hat and spring out of the darkness of alleyways upon befuddled drunks. His mind was as shadowy as the alleys he prowled and he needed psychiatric treatment. Psychiatrists, to be sure, do not have an answer for the problem of crime but they do contribute illuminating insights into the behavior of criminals. Yet there are only fifty professional psychiatrists among the 232 major federal and state prisons and reformatories. At other levels, trained personnel are also scarce, and except in a handful of prison systems, salaries are too low to attract competent people. Buildings too are generally rundown, obsolete, and jammed with prisoners.

Do most ex-convicts eventually return to prison? Are they as unredeemable as those who push for harsher penalties say they are? Certainly the ex-convict who wants to go straight can expect to have a rough time. When he leaves the walls he doesn't have money enough to last more than a few days. Many firms will not give him a job, at least if they know about his record. Sometimes even his family doesn't want anything to do with him. And in some cities the police will pick him up on any pretext, to put him into the day's "lineup" or merely to harass him so much that he'll move on to another town.

But the typical ex-prisoner persists in his efforts to surmount these difficulties. A five-year study of federal prisoners, done by the University of Illinois under a Ford Foundation grant, indicated that nine out of ten prisoners intend to take up an honest way of life when they get out. Some fail in their good intentions, but the same study proved that two-thirds are successful in staying out of trouble.

Our prison systems will not succeed in permanently "reforming" larger numbers of their graduates until communities are ready to play a much larger part in the rehabilitation process. And I wish that this problem would attract more serious attention and public discussion than, for example, the perennial emotional debate about capital punishment.

The issue here is between people who are certain that only the electric chair, the gas chamber, and the gallows protect us from an overwhelming horde of criminals, and others who consider these grim devices the stamp of a brutal and primitive society.

Today, it is chiefly the indigent, the friendless, the Negro, and the mentally ill who are doomed to death. . . . There should be an automatic psychiatric examination for everyone accused of a capital crime and an automatic appeal for everyone convicted of one. . . .

The pressures of our high-voltage society are too intense for many people to bear, and the consequence is too often a mental illness characterized by hostility toward one's fellowman. We need facilities for the treatment of the hostile, mentally ill persons who become involved in crime.

Currently, there is a trend to attack the crime problem by bringing the federal government more actively into the picture.

The fact is that when the federal government enters a field, the local and state authorities tend to abdicate. At the very least, misunderstandings and jealousies result which hobble law enforcement. The overlapping of criminal laws sends into federal prisons the physically handicapped, the alcoholic, and the other social misfits who are really the responsibility of local and state authorities.

THE GOAL IS NOT UTOPIA

Jurisdictional overlapping must be eliminated if agencies of different types and federal and state agencies are to work effectively together. At present the multiplication of law-enforcement and treatment agencies has made a morass out of the entire effort to combat crime.

Crime prevention . . . is a task for quiet, firm, persistent cooperative effort.

The fruit of such effort can be considerable. But it will not be a Utopia free of crime. Human beings are infinitely varied, and some of their behavior is bound to be considered criminal by at least a portion of society. The challenge we must meet is to reduce the basic causes of crime, improve law-enforcement methods, and use more effectively the techniques that have been developed for changing human behavior. The existence of crime and criminals should spur us on to experimentation, infuse new life into our efforts to rid the country of social injustices, and make us all a little more tolerant of each other's imperfect conduct.

What Do You Think?

1. How do you suppose Bishop Sheen (Reading 6), Arthur Miller (Reading 7), and Leonard Gross (Reading 8), in Chapter 4, would respond to Bennett's argument?

2. Bennett urges an automatic psychiatric examination for everyone accused of a capital crime and an automatic appeal for everyone convicted of one. Would you agree? Why or why not?

3. What is the strongest point in Bennett's argument? The weakest? Explain.

ACTIVITIES FOR INVOLVEMENT

1.　　Visit a nearby prison and interview the prison staff as to their views on capital punishment. Present for their reactions some of the points made by Allen and Brown.

2.　　Develop a questionnaire to ask a sample of people in your community concerning their views on capital punishment. Interview a variety of age groups, occupations, both sexes, etc., to obtain a good cross-section of opinion. What percentage of those interviewed argue for or against the death penalty? Now interview the members of your class. How do the results compare with the sample you obtained from the community at large? How would you explain any similarities or differences which appear?

3.　　Hold a round-table discussion on whether or not the death penalty is ever justified.

4.　　One of the strongest arguments for capital punishment is that the threat of death keeps people from committing murder and other capital crimes. The argument, in brief form, states that:

    a. People will refrain from committing crimes because they are afraid of being punished;

    b. Since people fear death more than anything else, the punishment most likely to prevent capital crimes is the death penalty.

What evidence could you present to support or refute this argument?

5.　　American criminal law divides offenders into two categories, "sane" and "insane." Insane defendants, under our system of justice, are judged "not guilty" and are sent to mental institutions. Legally "sane" defendants, when convicted, are sentenced to prison or death regardless of their mental condition. This division is based on the test of sanity laid down in the M'Naghten case of 1843: did the accused, at the time of the crime, know that his act was wrong and against the law?

Psychiatrists, on the other hand, hold that the "M'Naghten test" is outdated, since a tremendous amount of psychiatric knowledge has developed since 1843. They argue that knowledge of right and wrong alone is not an adequate test of a man's responsibility before the law, and the M'Naghten test does not allow for a variety of factors other than reason which affect and control human conduct. Modern psychiatry illustrates that men are mentally and emotionally unequal—and the mentally ill, therefore, do not have the same chance to lead law abiding lives as do those who are mentally healthy.

Do you think an individual might be mentally ill, yet still know that his actions are wrong and in violation of the law? Should insane persons be executed? How would you define insane?

6.　　Draw up a list of characteristics which you think a modern prison should display. Consider type of building, degree and nature of confinement, rules and regulations, administrative personnel, and supportive personnel needed, etc.

7.   In 1963 a Gallup survey sampled 171 communities across the nation. Respondents were asked how they would deal with a 17-year-old high school student from their own community who was caught stealing an automobile. They were told he had no previous record. Their responses were as follows, (a) being the response listed most often, (f) the response listed least often.

    a. Give him another chance, be lenient.

    b. Put him on probation; give him a suspended sentence.

    c. Put him under the care of a psychiatrist or social worker.

    d. Put him in an institution, jail, reformatory, etc.

    e. Release him in the custody of his parents.

    f. Punish his parents, fine them.

Would you differ with this order in any way? Explain. Would you add any other suggestions to the list?

8.   Many authorities on crime feel there are two ways to reduce crime. One way is to head off crime by working with young people to show them that nothing can be gained through a life of crime. Another way is to strengthen law enforcement agencies to make it very difficult for criminals to get away with crime. Suppose you had to choose between these two ways, which one would you favor: trying to stop criminals before they begin or strengthening the police force to crack down on crime?

BIBLIOGRAPHY
For Further Study

Books

BROMBERG, WALTER · *Crime and the Mind* · New York, N. Y.: The Macmillan Co., 1965.

CHESSMAN, CARYL · *Cell 2455, Death Row* · Englewood Cliffs, N. J.: Prentice-Hall, 1954.

COLEBROOK, JOAN · *The Cross of Lassitude: Portraits of Five Juvenile Delinquents* · New York, N. Y.: Alfred A. Knopf, 1967.

CONRAD, JOHN P. · *Crime and Its Correction: An International Survey of Attitudes and Practices* · Berkeley and Los Angeles: Univ. of California Press, 1965.

CRESSEY, DONALD R. (ed.) · *The Prison* · New York, N. Y.: Holt, Rinehart & Winston, 1961.

Crime and Justice in America · Washington, D. C.: Congressional Quarterly Service, August, 1967.

GENTRY, CURT · *The Vulnerable Americans* · Garden City, N. Y.: Doubleday & Co., 1966.

GIBBONS, DON C. · *Changing the Lawbreaker: The Treatment of Delinquents and Criminals* · Englewood Cliffs, N. J.: Prentice-Hall, 1965.

HALLECK, SEYMOUR · *Psychiatry and the Dilemmas of Crime* · New York, N. Y.: Harper & Row, 1967.

LOTH, DAVID · *Crime in the Suburbs* · New York, N. Y.: William Morrow & Co., 1967.

LUNDEN, WALTER ALBIN · *Crimes and Criminals* · Ames, Iowa: Iowa State Univ. Press, 1967.

MIKES, GEORGE, (ed.) · *Prison* · New York, N. Y.: Horizon Press, 1964.

RICCIO, VINCENT and BILL SLOCUM · *All the Way Down: The Violent Underworld of Street Gangs* · New York, N. Y.: Simon and Schuster, 1962.

SUTHERLAND, EDWIN H. · *White Collar Crime* · New York, N. Y.: The Dryden Press, 1949.

TUNLEY, ROUL · *Kids, Crimes and Chaos* · New York, N. Y.: Harper & Row, 1962.

U. S. FEDERAL BUREAU OF INVESTIGATION · *Uniform Crime Reports for the United States* · Washington, D. C.: U. S. Government Printing Office. Published annually.

U. S. PRESIDENT'S COMMISSION ON LAW ENFORCEMENT AND ADMINISTRATION OF JUSTICE · *The Challenge of Crime in a Free Society* · Washington, D. C.: U. S. Government Printing Office, February, 1967.

WHITEHEAD, DON · *The FBI Story* · New York, N. Y.: Random House, 1956.

Paperback Books

BEDAU, HUGO ADAM · *The Death Penalty in America: An Anthology* · Chicago, Ill.: Aldine Publishing Co. (Also published as a Doubleday Anchor Original paperback.)

FRANK, JEROME · *Courts on Trial: Myth and Reality in American Justice* · Chicago, Ill.: Atheneum.

FRANKFURTER, FELIX · *Case of Sacco and Vanzetti* · New York, N. Y.: Grosset & Dunlap (Universal Library).

HAUSE, BRANT, (ed.) · *Great Trials of Famous Lawyers* · New York, N. Y.: Ace Books.

HIBBERT, C. · *The Roots of Evil* · New York, N. Y.: Penguin Books.

HIRSCH, P. · *Cop* · New York, N.Y.: Pyramid.

KVARACEUS, W. C. · *Dynamics of Delinquency* · Englewood Cliffs, N. J.: Prentice-Hall.

LLOYD, DENNIS · *The Idea of Law* · New York, N. Y.: Penguin Books.

SMITH, ANN D. · *Women in Prison* · Chicago, Ill.: Quadrangle.

SUTHERLAND, E. H. · *The Professional Thief* · Chicago, Ill.: Phoenix Books.

THRASHER, F. M. · *The Gang* · Chicago, Ill.: Atheneum.

WEINBERG, ARTHUR (ed.) · *Attorney for the Damned* · New York, N. Y.: Simon and Schuster.

WEST, D. J. · *Young Offender* · New York, N. Y.: Penguin Books.

WEST, REBECCA · *The New Meaning of Treason* · New York, N. Y.: Viking Press (Compass Books).

WHYTE, W. F. · *Street Corner Society* · Chicago, Ill.: Atheneum.

WIRTH, L. · *The Ghetto* · Chicago, Ill.: Phoenix Books.

Articles

ALEXANDER, M. E. · "What Life Is Like in Today's Federal Prisons," *U. S. News and World Report*, Vol. 61, July 14, 1966.

ALGREN, NELSON · "Down With Cops," *The Saturday Evening Post,* October 23, 1965.

ANONYMOUS · "Have You Ever Been Convicted of a Felony?" *Reader's Digest,* September, 1965.

BAILEY, RONALD · "Facing Death, a New Life Perhaps Too Late," *Life,* Vol. 53, July 27, 1962.

BISHOP, G. W. · "Four and a Half Days in Atlanta's Jails," *Atlantic,* Vol. 214, July, 1964.

COLES, ROBERT · "The Question of Negro Crime," *Harper's Magazine,* April, 1964.

"Cop Watching: The Need for a Code to Guide Police," *The New Republic,* Vol. 155, December 3, 1966.

Crime and Delinquency, Vol. 9, October, 1963 · Entire issue given over to articles on the Model Sentencing Act.

CROMIE, R. · "Chance to Go Straight," *The Saturday Evening Post,* Vol. 232, April 30, 1960.

FOONER, M. · "Crime and Affluence: Case of the Culpable Victim," *The Nation,* March 6, 1967.

INBAU, F. E. · "Behind Those Police Brutality Charges," *Reader's Digest,* Vol. 89, July, 1966.

JOHNSON, PAMELA HANSFORD · "Who's to Blame When a Murder Strikes?" *Life,* Vol. 61, August 12, 1966.

MCCORD, W. M. · "We Ask the Wrong Questions About Crime," *The New York Times Magazine,* November 21, 1965.

MAROSSI, RUTH and GERALD KREFETZ · "Philadelphia: Policing the Police," *The Reporter,* Vol. 27, July 19, 1962.

METHWIN, E. H. · "Let's Have Justice for Non-Criminals Too," *Reader's Digest,* Vol. 89, December, 1966.

MONTAGUE, ASHLEY · "The Biologist Looks at Crime," *Annals of the American Academy of Political and Social Science,* CCXVII, September, 1941.

PEARMAN, R. · "Arkansas Prison Farm: The Whip Pays Off," *The Nation,* Vol. 203, December 26, 1966.

PIERCE, PONCHITTA · "Crime in the Suburbs," *Ebony,* August, 1965.

SCHILLER, ANDREW · "People in Trouble," *Harper's Magazine,* April, 1964.

SLATER, SIDNEY · "My Life Inside The Mob," *The Saturday Evening Post,* August 24–31, 1963.

TRASK, ROBERT A. · "The Waiting Time," *Harper's Magazine,* April, 1964.

"U.S. Crime: Its Scope and Causes," *Current History,* June, 1967, entire issue.

"U.S. Crime and Law Enforcement," *Current History,* July, 1967, entire issue.

"U.S. Crime: Punishment and Prevention," *Current History,* August, 1967, entire issue.

Films, Filmstrips, Tapes

Ask Me, Don't Tell Me by David Myers for the American Friends Service Committee (22 min; B/W; 1960) · Unique, positive approach for reaching juvenile delinquents. Made in San Francisco.

The Criminal Man: Brakes and Misbehavior (30 min; B/W; prod. NET-KQED) · Relates criminal behavior to the lack or failure of psychological controls on energies and impulses.

The Criminal Man: Crime Under Twenty-One (30 min; B/W; prod. NET-KQED) · Discusses criminal behavior of teenagers, pointing out that the extent of juvenile delinquency may be exaggerated and showing how improvements in statistics, reporting, and apprehension influence total picture of teenage crime. Presents a group of young people discussing themselves and their problems.

The Criminal Man: The Criminal and How to Neutralize Him (30 min; B/W; prod. NET-KQED) · Discusses the need for a constructive program for criminal rehabilitation, pointing out that a true correctional philosophy has not been formulated. Includes a scale model of an ideal correctional system. Stresses the desirability of a program for convict evaluation and subsequent treatment.

The Criminal Man: The Criminal and Punishment (30 min; B/W; prod. NET-KQED) · Discusses concept of punishment of criminal behavior and explains the evolution of rehabilitation with emphasis on the criminal rather than the crime. Includes a visit to a cell block in San Quentin where five inmates are interviewed.

The Criminal Man: Culture and Crime (30 min; B/W; prod. NET-KQED) · Analyzes patterns of culture and their influence on the rise of criminality, using the Nazi regime in Germany as an example. Points out how accepted behavior in one culture may be a crime in another. Discusses impact of cultures meeting headon, thus giving rise to criminal behavior.

The Criminal Man: The Ethnological Criminal (30 min; B/W; prod. NET-KQED) · Discusses relationship of crime to race, national origin, and minority groups, pointing out patterns of belief and the misconceptions that exist. Relates living conditions and geographical distribution to crime, and concludes that race is irrelevant to criminality.

Crime—Everybody's Problem (36 fr.; prod. Wayne State Univ.) · Causes, prevention of crime, rehabilitation methods, cost of law enforcement.

Crime in the Streets (60 min; B/W; prod. NET) · About 50 per cent of all serious street crime is committed by boys under 18. This film examines two aspects of juvenile crime, the quality of police protection, and programs for rehabilitation of offenders.

Criminology (27 min; Univ. of California "Search" series) · Modern study of criminology. What is being done to get convicts back into civilian life.

The Forbidden Name of Wednesday (Tape; 30 min; 1953; Series: Ways of Mankind) · A study of tribal methods in dealing with crime and punishment among the Ashanti of Ghana.

The Hangman by Paul Julian and M. Ogden (12 min; color; 1964; dist. Contemporary) · Prizewinning animated film. Allegory of injustice and moral responsibility which could, among other things, be interpreted as an attack on capital punishment.

Hooked (20 min; B/W; 1966, dist. Churchill Films) · Narcotic's corrosive effects on mental, physical, and emotional states are dramatically revealed when young former drug addicts tell why they began addiction and the futility of life while hooked. Filmed in prisons and Synanon centers in California.

House on the Beach (60 min; B/W; prod. NET) · One of the new developments in the rehabilitation of drug addicts is the communal center approach at Synanon (Santa Monica, California) which emphasizes self-help among volunteer addicts working and living together.

In King County, Washington (Tape; 30 min; prod. Univ. of Colorado, National Tape Repository) · King County, Washington, reorganizes court system to meet juvenile problem.

The Local Police and Prevention of Juvenile Delinquency (Racial Tensions and Delinquency) (Parts 1 and 2) (Tape; 60 min; Univ. of Colorado, National Tape Repository) · How school is working with others in community to help gain, enhance respect due law enforcers.

Oregon State Penitentiary (Parts 1 and 2 from Series "In Our Care"; 30 min each part; B/W; dist. Oregon State Univ., Corvallis, Oregon) · Procedure followed in admitting a prisoner to the Oregon State Penitentiary. Show physical and mental study of each new inmate. Rehabilitation through industrial jobs carried out in the Oregon state prison. Vocational training of inmates. Prison farm annex, officer's training program, camp program for inmates. Segregation of difficult prisoners. Women's section.

Probation Officer (32 min; B/W; made in Britain; dist. by Contemporary Films, N. Y.) · How probation officers are trained and work in England to help young delinquents. One family with delinquent girl shown; how probation officer works with her, family, court to restore child to society.

The Quiet One (2 reels; 67 min; B/W; 1948; prod. Film Documents, Inc.) · The classic study of a mentally disturbed Negro boy, victim of disrupted home. Sent to Wiltwyck School at age ten; receives therapy and emotional comfort, sets him on the path of rehabilitation.

Stand-In for a Murderer (Tape; 30 min; 1952; Series: Ways of Mankind) · A study of Indian culture in S. E. Alaska, revolving around ritual combat.

The Story of Andy (Case Histories) (Tape; Univ. of Colorado; 19 min. 30 sec) · Man, aged 33, tells what he did after running away at age 13, recalls pressures that led him to drinking.

Who Killed Michael Farmer? (Tape; 63 min; 1958) · Interviews by Edward R. Murrow. Parents interviewed on how and why their son was murdered by gang of hoodlums in New York, 1957. Gang members interviewed for reactions to murder.